Modern Ma

This is a book about how to swim with the sharks while living like a dolphin. It provides a unique mix of cunning and integrity—as if Machiavelli and Stephen Covey got together and wrote a book on the rules for living. Without being either pessimistic or cynical, the book deals with some hard truths about human nature that we ignore at our peril. The authors' advice is both practical and tactical on topics such as dealing with conflict, office politics, difficult personalities, and not letting others take advantage of you. Master these techniques and you'll be adept at handling the worst in others, while strengthening what's best in yourself.

Tim Ward, author of *Indestructible You* and *The Master Communicator's Handbook*

Every person experiencing interpersonal conflict or cut-throat competition should read this book. I have personally benefited from Dr. Bruner's consultation and highly recommend his book. It is the opposite of psycho-babble: concrete, specific, and dynamic.

Robert W. Forster, President and CEO, Forster Financial

Modern Machiavelli provides key insights and inspiration to propel your life dramatically forward!

William Eager, speaker, corporate strategist and best-selling author

Modern Machiavelli: 13 Laws of Power, Persuasion and Integrity is a book that crosses the areas of business, psychology, self-help, and ethics. It is a realist's manual for effective persuasion and conflict management.

Christine Joo, Ed.D., Christine Joo Psychotherapy

Dr. Bruner and Philip Eager have provided a much-needed treatise on the basic behavioral "laws" that all of us need to fully understand if we are to truly work together to solve the many issues facing society. This book is not designed to show you how to manipulate co-workers, friends, and family members, but rather provides the reader with a strategic awareness of the many facets that may be in play when individuals interact, regardless of the situation. This book is a must for the reader who is interested in a layman's dive into moral development and offers approaches, through professional insight and examples, on how to uphold the "fairness" expectations that many of us have grown up with, without compromising our core values that make us who we are.

David White, Ph.D., Associate Dean of Research, University of Tennessee

Modern Machiavelli

13 Laws of Power, Persuasion and Integrity

Modern Machiavelli

13 Laws of Power, Persuasion
and Integrity

Troy Bruner and Philip Eager

CHANGE
MAKERS
BOOKS

Winchester, UK
Washington, USA

First published by Changemakers Books, 2017
Changemakers Books is an imprint of John Hunt Publishing Ltd., Laurel House, Station Approach,
Alresford, Hants, SO24 9JH, UK
office1@jhpbooks.net
www.johnhuntpublishing.com
www.changemakers-books.com

For distributor details and how to order please visit the 'Ordering' section on our website.

Text copyright: Troy Bruner and Philip Eager 2016

ISBN: 978 1 78535 611 7
978 1 78535 612 4 (ebook)
Library of Congress Control Number: 2016954752

A CIP catalogue record for this book is available from the British Library.

Design: Stuart Davies

Printed and bound by CPI Group (UK) Ltd, Croydon, CR0 4YY, UK

We operate a distinctive and ethical publishing philosophy in all
areas of our business, from our global network of authors to
production and worldwide distribution.

CONTENTS

To Susan, Wendy, and our clients and colleagues
for their vital contributions

Preface

The authors of this book are strategic consultants with backgrounds in psychotherapy. In our work with individuals, couples, business owners and employees, we have noticed a pattern of problems that is seldom researched within academia or any specific discipline including psychology, business management, and ethics. We have studied and learned that under certain circumstances many highly desirable and prosocial human qualities can undermine an individual's efforts to achieve career and relational success. Think of any desirable quality, such as persistence, reliability, generosity, loyalty, etc. These qualities are not necessarily advantageous when interacting with individuals that outwardly conform to social expectations, but in reality are willing to act deceptively or manipulatively when it is to their advantage. People who genuinely try to live according to standards of conduct tend to become demoralized when they realize that their efforts to achieve goals and find success have been sabotaged by the selfish actions of others.

Those who have difficulty detecting and responding to deception or manipulation usually find themselves exasperated. The most common response is to settle for less than deserved in the name of "compromise," or worse, choosing to abandon one's ambitions altogether. Imagine what a loss it would have been if Abraham Lincoln had decided, "Politics is too corrupt. I'm just going to run my little law office and stay out of it. Let someone else run for office." Society, like Nature, abhors a vacuum. When those with personal integrity walk away from success, others gladly fill in the void. On the other hand, when people of personal integrity succeed, the subsequent good that is accomplished can have ripple effects that positively impact the lives of countless individuals.

The core aspects of life such as family, career, and personal growth can be frustrated by the selfishness of those around us. The inability to respond effectively can result in conflict, depression, anxiety, and frustration. But such problems are much less likely for those who master the art and science of engaging selfishness in its many subtle forms: exploitation, manipulation, deceit, betrayal, etc. We must accept that our social world includes many individuals who do not hesitate to act in their own selfish interests, even when it materially or psychologically harms others. In fact, there is merit to the thesis that selfishness is the primary, indirect cause of human suffering. On an individual level, proper social strategy is both protection against selfishness and empowerment for success.

There are of course the "others"; the "salt of the earth" parents, co-workers, and friends who are supportive, empathetic, and kind. Many individuals have had the good fortune of surrounding themselves with such positive people. However, the authors of this book do not believe this group represents the majority of the most successful individuals in every environment. The path to "success" is often associated with a competitive attitude, ambition, and strength of will. Some individuals with these qualities are wonderful people; others are willing to succeed at all costs. Usually where there is more money, power, or status, there will be more corruption, predatory competition, and deceit. On the other hand, even petty things or extremely limited power can be associated with "power trips" including attempts to dominate or exploit others. Despite these observations, there is no easy way to read others. *Selfishness can take subtle forms across a wide spectrum of human experience.* Our world is a mix of vices and virtues; joy and pain; loyalty and betrayal. The preoccupation of the authors is to help others discover a path to overcoming oppressive forces in order to succeed in life and attain a high level of confidence in social interactions.

This book is more than just about helping others learn how to cope. "Coping" means the ability to endure suffering or at best rising above it—doubtless worthy and necessary goals—but to be truly successful more is needed than calm endurance: it requires an active repertoire of strategies for engaging oppressive forces and overcoming situational difficulties. On a grand scale, the world does not need more selfish successful people, but all it takes for them to succeed is for good people to give up and let others reap the rewards and accomplishments that were abandoned because it was "just too hard." *Many excellent books have been written about how to think strategically, but virtually none of them speaks solely to the person of integrity; that is, the person who is generally well-intentioned and genuinely cares for the welfare of others.*

Success in life does not depend upon whether you are wicked or angelic. Many individuals with entirely selfish or even highly destructive designs have been successful in this world. But if you desire to attain your own version of "success" in life, then you must learn how to become wise in the ways of the world without compromising your integrity. This is very difficult because the advantageous thing to do is not always the right thing to do. Other people around you might be selfish and unconcerned with your feelings. If you are a lover of peace, you must learn how to battle oppression; if you are trusting, you must learn appropriate cautiousness; if you are honest, then you must learn selective disclosure. If you are generous, empathetic, loyal, or possess any of the qualities of a moral person, none of this will come naturally to you. But take heart; there is a way to become successful without losing your soul. In fact, the world might depend upon it.

The content of this book is not easy to implement. It will require review, practice, adjustment, risk-taking, and skill. The task at hand is to identify what you have been doing wrong and how to implement a corrective strategy. But prior to that, you need to assess yourself and see whether or not you have the skills and temperament to think strategically and follow through with effective implementation. If you cannot control your emotions, you will not be able to be consistent enough in your actions to be strategic in the long term. In addition, you need to be able to be subtle. You must be calm and graceful because success is more likely when others cannot easily anticipate your actions. There is no quick remedy for dealing with selfish people and no easy answer for every problematic situation, but with consistency and patience, even a very cautious strategy can produce big gains.

It is also important to learn about human personality and motivation. If you can discern what motivates someone, you can anticipate the general direction of their behavior. You must be able to perceive situations from different perspectives by imagining what it is like to be someone else with different values and how they might interpret any given situation. Finally, you must possess the skill of anticipating possibilities. While no one can predict the future, if you can hypothesize various outcomes you will reduce your chances of being surprised by events when they occur and you can have a ready plan available to respond in the best way possible.

Most of the best books about strategic engagement have been written by generals, princes, corporate titans or for those who aspire to such statuses, but in the modern world, even the most capable and ambitious individuals will never fit these descriptions. It is less important whether someone achieves a grandiose dream; the more important thing is to achieve optimally in every situation while keeping one's integrity. At the end of each chapter the reader is encouraged to take a personal inventory which includes *testing your knowledge, changing something,* and *developing wisdom*.

One final note: this book describes several real-life experiences of individuals who sought professional help for a variety of problems. Critical details have been changed to make them unidentifiable. Fictional examples and anecdotes written to make a point do not include the words "real-life example."

Introduction

"Why am I not getting ahead in life while the self-centered people I know seem to get promoted, make more money, and have more friends than me?"

"How do I deal with clever but highly selfish people?"

"How do I not only survive but thrive in competitive situations?"

"How do I disarm critics and win people to my point of view?"

"Is there a way to present a positive image to others without losing my authenticity?"

"How can I detect deception and avoid manipulation?"

"How do I stand my ground with people that are more assertive than me?"

"Why am I loyal to others, but others are not loyal to me when it counts?"

"How should I deal with conflict?"

If one or more of these questions resonates with you, then you need to know that there is a way to change your life by mastering the skill and art of strategic engagement. You can get what you want and keep what you have *without sacrificing your core values*. Stop living a life that accommodates disappointment and pain. This book will help you learn how to manage difficult people and fix your relationships in your personal and professional life. But changing your life cannot happen unless you are willing to change something about yourself. Now is the time to stop blaming others (even when they deserve it) and embrace smarter, strategic ways to engage social reality.

But let us wind back the clock. There was probably a time when you believed in yourself and had hopes and ideals about your future. But over the years, blow after blow of disappointment detached you from your old aspirations and desires. Perhaps you are discouraged and overly critical of yourself. Perhaps others have let you down in some big, damaging ways. Maybe you have decided that happiness is a myth. Maybe "this is just how life is." Now is the time to rebuild your confidence, find your personal power, reconnect with your inner "fire," and begin living up to your true potential.

Chapter 1

Law 1: Expect Others to Act from Self-Interest

When asked, "Is there one word that may serve as a rule of practice for all one's life?" he answered, "Is not reciprocity such a word?"
— *Analects of Confucius*

Everyone has self-interests—you, your co-workers, friends, family, and everyone you know have their own interests and desires. Even people who dedicate their lives to serving others use their resources to advance something they care about. There is absolutely nothing wrong with self-interest. In fact, someone who makes sure his or her emotional, financial, and relational needs are met can be of great benefit to others. The happiness of others is also part of self-interest. We want our loved ones to be happy, and when they suffer, we suffer. On a wider social level, we remain mindful about the well-being of others in society, even as we try to meet our own needs and desires. This is sometimes called "enlightened self-interest." *Self-interest is the key to understanding human motivation and behavior.*

Self-Interest Is Not Selfishness

Self-interest becomes selfishness whenever someone desires something and is willing to disregard others in order to get it. Selfish people are self-interested, but at the exclusion of others. As an example, it might be in my self-interest to wait in line for something, but if I push someone else out of the way to move up in line, then my self-interest has become selfish. In the "real" world—whether at home, school, work, or within a social group—you are likely to encounter over time many selfish individuals. Sometimes it is easy to notice selfishness and take precautions; at other times, it is subtle. There are those who appear civil, but in their minds and hearts do not care about the welfare of others, unless it is to their advantage. Many people are latently selfish; that is, like a hibernating bear, their selfishness is temporarily dormant. As long as things are going well, the bear might not awaken. But under the right circumstances, someone's desire for personal gain will become more important to them than anything about you. When this happens, the person you thought you knew as your friend, colleague, or life partner can cause you significant emotional and material damage.

Success Requires Engagement

In the process of advancing your career, developing relationships, and attempts to find personal happiness, you are likely to encounter many selfish individuals. Some will be overly critical, disloyal, deceitful, and even hostile. Many selfish people are like sharks; they look for weaknesses and prey upon vulnerabilities. This fact is not limited to pathological people like psychopaths and narcissists—many ordinary people, under the right circumstances, can act with total disregard for others. When this happens, the ones you trusted most will have caused the most damage. If you have ever been betrayed, manipulated, or deceived, then you probably do not want it to happen again. If you have ever been blindsided by toxic personalities, then you probably want to respond better next time. Success in life depends upon being able to swim with the sharks without getting bitten; integrity means not becoming a shark yourself, even when it seems advantageous.

Engagement Is Better Than Avoidance

Personal and career goals, especially if you aim high, require effective social strategies. It is not enough to simply avoid or control "difficult people." Those who merely try to avoid difficult people might sometimes be successful only to later find themselves at a huge disadvantage due to inexperience. Avoidance can also be perceived by others as an indication of fear, lack of confidence, or social incompetence. Attempting to control others is another poor strategy. Most of us do not have the requisite authority or power to coerce others, but even when this is possible, if hearts and minds are not influenced, others will passive-aggressively work behind the scenes to undermine your efforts. You cannot control others or change the world, but you can choose to learn to optimally respond to circumstances in a way that engenders success; success, in turn, allows a person to maximize their positive contributions to the world, which might, in a small way, promote the advancement of humankind.

Who Are Selfish People?

There are two broad groups of selfish individuals that can be broken down into subtypes. The first group includes those who are chronically selfish and have negative intentions toward those who get in their way: the narcissists, psychopaths, sadists, pretentious, passive-aggressive, and dramatic. These types are discussed in detail in Chapter 2 and we refer to such individuals as *antagonistic personalities* (we emphasize that personality is the problem, not the person). Antagonistic personalities are characterized by a willingness to get their way by manipulating or victimizing others. In some ways these individuals can be easier to manage because they tend to be highly predictable.

The second category includes the *weakly virtuous*. These are individuals who at their core know right from wrong, and might even act decently 99% of the time, but at some point they can turn on you if it is to their advantage. This type can cause you the most pain if you are not careful because they might have earned your trust or friendship only to throw it away when the temptation is right. But remember not to demonize people who act selfishly. Human weakness is a core reason people—

sometimes even really good people—fail to live up to their own ideals and "sell you down the river" to get ahead. What tends to make the weakly virtuous selfish and willing to manipulate or exploit others includes the following:

- Strong social pressure to conform
- Fear or insecurity
- Temptations too hard to resist
- High levels of stress
- Highly competitive environments
- Psychological problems, such as depression, addiction, or personality disorders
- The belief that someone is superior to others (narcissism)
- Lack of a conscience
- Sadism: getting pleasure out of someone else's pain

Ultimately, the reason this or that person is selfish is far less important than how to respond in a way that is simultaneously protective and advantageous. Whether you encounter selfishness from weak, damaged, or malicious people, your task is to avoid becoming a victim. One very important step in this process is to understand that the core Self of another person might be radically different from your core Self. Consider the following thought experiment: if you forced yourself to act selfishly at someone else's expense, would it bother you? Most likely it would. But there are probably at least one or two people you know who would barely—if at all—become bothered by their own selfish actions.

The Reciprocity Distortion

Reciprocity: a situation or relationship in which two people or groups agree to do something similar for each other, to allow each other to have the same rights; a reciprocal arrangement

or relationship.
—*Merriam-Webster Dictionary*

Reciprocity is the glue that underlies our relationships with others and holds societies together. From a young age we are instructed to be social and to expect fairness in relationships. We are taught that life is like a two-way street where our displays of niceness, fairness, favors, hard work, and respect will be reciprocated back to us from others. Some related popular sayings include: "Respect others and they will respect you." "Work hard and you will be noticed." "Be nice and others will grow to like you." "If you are loyal to others, they will be loyal to you." As adults, if we do someone a favor, we expect that most of the time the other person will have the impulse to eventually repay the favor. We try to live by some version of the statement, "Treat other people the way that you want to be treated."

Some of us were fortunate enough to grow up in neighborhoods where favors were exchanged all the time. For example, when an elderly neighbor was sick, maybe a neighbor mowed her lawn. Later on, that elderly neighbor might have fed that family's dog after they left on vacation. In such neighborhoods there are no written rules about exchanging favors—it comes naturally. "You scratch my back, and I'll scratch yours." Sometimes an unasked favor was done just to express goodwill or to make someone happy. Thankfully there remain many people and places like this in the world today where reciprocity is alive and well; even better, where sometimes people are altruistic and expect nothing in return for helping others.

These are examples of reciprocity and for most of human history reciprocity has been a highly successful social expectation. Reciprocity has been the faith behind our ability to exchange goods, share resources, and make treaties. Laws and contracts are based on expectations about fairness and reciprocity. Most of us are not even conscious of how powerful reciprocity is in the human mind and how it influences our behavior on a daily basis. In fact, there are many social rules that make society work and influence our decisions and actions. As we go through life perhaps we might become a little more cynical about people, but expectations for reciprocity remain internally powerful. We always hope for reciprocity, even when we are not sure we can trust someone. People tend to operate on a "default" reciprocity mindset, expecting it as the norm. Psychologists call this the *reciprocity bias*.

But reciprocity fails when selfish people pursue their own desires at the expense of others. In competitive work environments and complex romantic entanglements many of us suddenly discover that we have been interacting with selfish people who have not reciprocated our good intentions or sense of fairness. Sadly, it is not uncommon for someone's own family to be torn apart by selfishness. It can be incredibly stressful and emotional when even one family member attempts to exploit or manipulate their own parents, siblings, or extended family.

It is even more common for one or more of our co-workers to use manipulation or deceit to attain some advantage over others. Sometimes such individuals are highly successful. It seems unfair when selfish people with shark-like mentalities get ahead in life because they are ruthless.

What happens to so many of us is that we play fair, only to be mistreated by people who, quite frankly, do not give a damn about anything but their own needs and wants. They act concerned, but really look after their own self-interests at work or in relationships. They are willing to act deceptively and manipulatively in order to get ahead; in the process they expend great effort to conceal their intentions and appear socially acceptable. For such people, selfishness usually overshadows genuine good works and the real positive qualities of character: honesty, trust, respect, forgiveness, responsibility, fairness, and caring. Even a single person who decides to not live by the "rules" can cause major damage in relationships, careers, and our emotions.

The natural reaction to these sentiments is to become increasingly cynical and defensive. In such a world, is it possible to achieve personal and professional goals with integrity? If you believe that it is hard to get ahead in life with integrity, then you are probably making some mistakes. There is a way to swim with the sharks without getting eaten or becoming a shark yourself. Of course there are times when it really does not benefit someone to "do the right thing," but there are a lot of mistakes and false assumptions good people make that result in totally unnecessary failures. If you are tired of not getting ahead in life despite your excellent personal qualities, then keep reading. There is a way to be successful without compromising your integrity. An important step is to get rid of false and misleading beliefs about yourself and others. Scrutinize the following laws and read the following stories and observations to see if they make sense to you. Think about how to apply the principles of this book to the difficult situations and people you have encountered.

The Dark Side of Reciprocity

Reciprocity is only successful when both parties act according to prosocial values like justice and fairness. But the difference between actually *valuing* being prosocial versus *pretending* to be prosocial is important. When it really counts no one ever admits, "I am acting selfishly."

Dealing with people is like being a member of the King's court in olden times: outwardly everyone plays by the rules, but inwardly many plot to remove their competition and obtain favor from those above them. We are foolish to not expect selfishness and to assume that others will share our values and play fair. As noted earlier, even "good" people that are not ordinarily selfish are likely to turn on someone under certain circumstances. Even when we have established, long-term relationships with others, reciprocity can become a dangerous expectation. When circumstances are just right, due to moral weakness or intense emotions, even "good" people are vulnerable to violating the rights of others in order to obtain an advantage.

It is even more dangerous to expect reciprocity from someone who is able to cleverly conceal their selfishness. A sophisticated manipulator will perceive reciprocity as a weakness, as something to be exploited as they advance their own self-centered agenda. By the time someone catches on, significant damage may have already been done. Since none of us can see into the soul of another person, we cannot easily detect the selfish intentions of shrewd, intelligent people. It is therefore safest to dispense with expectations about reciprocity altogether.

Can trust, goodwill, and fairness be relied upon in the context of well-established, proven relationships? Of course these are elements of our confidence in others. But it is *always* risky. Consider the following facts:

- In the United States approximately half of marriages end in divorce.
- Due to interpersonal conflict, the majority of people are permanently estranged from at least one family member.
- In recent years several highly respected companies with long track records have failed due to financial corruption.

Just because someone has been trustworthy *so far*, or even loves you, does not mean that they will never act selfishly at your expense—nobody is perfect. After the fact, it may still be possible to repair relationships. Little things are easily forgiven; after all, no one is a selfless angel. But life is not a game where we should take unnecessary risks. It is better to be cautious than get burned. Therefore, it is necessary to learn the skills that are simultaneously protective from harm yet proactively increase the odds of interpersonal success.

Vulnerability Factors

Let us explore some of the ways that the values underlying reciprocity can undermine someone's success by making them vulnerable to manipulation and exploitation.

We assume that most people are well-intentioned until proven otherwise

This assumption is often wrong. Many people disguise their selfish intentions but outwardly appear to play by the rules of society. People do not disclose socially unacceptable motivations such as greed, lust, pride, or a desire to dominate or exact revenge upon others.

We assume that disagreements can be worked out

Most people try to be rational and willing to compromise. Unfortunately, hidden agendas motivate some people to prefer winning at all costs over compromise.

We put effort into keeping our word and expect the same

When honest and dishonest persons interact, the honest person can be at a disadvantage. Those willing to break their word will do so when it is to their advantage. Deception is sometimes difficult to detect and not realized until after damage has been done.

We reciprocate based on fairness

Returning favors, cooperation, and other social obligations are based on expectations for reciprocity. A deceptive person might act reciprocally at first, only to later act selfishly.

We are capable of empathy

The ability to sense what someone else is feeling and imagine what that is like is required for compassion and concern.

Emotions are sometimes prime targets for manipulation.

We tend to be prosocial

Moral individuals tend to consider the good of all, respect authority, and follow rules. They want to be liked and respected. Selfish individuals outwardly adhere to prosocial values when convenient, but opportunistically violate or exploit social conventions at the expense of others. Some people consider other people as merely a means to an end.

We tend to be idealistic

An idealistic person is prone to seeing gaps between how the world is and how it should be. An exploitative person will prey upon the hopes and dreams of an idealistic person without caring about social harmony.

Replace Reciprocity with Personal Integrity

Many people are confused about what kind of expectations they should have about people in general. Many of us have an idealistic focus upon how people *should* act, which disappoints, rather than *how* people act in reality. Regardless of expectations, all social engagement is risky because it is impossible to read minds and have absolute certainty about the motives of others. It is therefore critical to develop new ways of thinking and reacting based upon strategy rather than making automatic assumptions about people or responding emotionally. Proper social strategy is especially important when we encounter highly selfish persons or antagonistic personalities. But what can replace our assumptions about others based on reciprocity? What mindset can protect us from selfish individuals without it resulting in paranoia?

Reciprocity values need to be replaced with *personal integrity*. *Personal integrity* is a prism with which to view others that is realistic and can replace faulty assumptions. It is a principle that prioritizes your values. It is a foundation for moving forward on your way to adopting more sophisticated ideas about social strategy.

Personal Integrity Principles:

A) A person is only responsible for his or her own intentions, not those of others.

B) No one can know with 100% certainty the intentions of another person; therefore, when interacting with people it is best to assume the possibility of negative or positive intentions.

C) Successful social engagement does not necessarily depend upon personal integrity. Many people without integrity have been successful.

D) Despite C, someone can become highly successful and achieve their goals by using effective strategies and methods that do not require the sacrifice of personal integrity.

Focus on Things You Can Control; Detach from Expectations

The personal responsibility principle above, A, states that "a person is only responsible for his or her own intentions." How do you let go of your expectations of others and focus on doing the right thing? The best way to do this is to break things down into two questions: 1) what is your responsibility? And, 2) what is the other person's responsibility? You have control over 1, but not 2. Focus on what you need to do, and how you need to respond to others, but detach from worrying about the rights and wrongs of the actions of others. This mindset is critical; without it, the actions and attitudes of selfish people will result in anxiety, anger, demoralization, and frustration. *When our happiness depends entirely upon the actions of others, we no longer have control over our life.* We are like a boat without oars, responding to the circumstances caused by others, without the ability to control our own destiny.

In general, we as individuals are responsible for the following:

- Keeping our own expectations realistic
- Our words
- Our actions
- How we respond to problems
- Our intentions
- Our willingness to be fair, generous, and loyal
- Our preferences
- Our best efforts to attain success

We as individuals are not responsible for the following:

- Whether or not others live up to our expectations
- The words of others
- The actions of others
- The decisions of others
- The intentions of others
- Whether others are fair, generous, or loyal
- The preferences of others
- People willing to interfere with our success

People with morals and ideals often become entrapped by their own standards. They look around and see a huge gap between how the world is and how it "should" be: "People should be less selfish." "People should use common sense." "People should be compassionate." This entire schema of thinking in terms of "should" is flawed and based upon self-invented rules. Imagine how silly it would be if someone said, "The universe should be different than it is right now." "Should" really means "I prefer

___" or "I would like ___" Replace "should" with these kinds of statements and you will more accurately describe what you are really thinking. Did someone act selfishly? Then you would have *preferred* otherwise, but this is not within your control.

Imagine the absurdity of the reverse: someone imposing their standards upon you. Would it make sense for someone to tell you, "You should" do this or that, as if they made rules for your life? People tend to make even bad choices because they think it is in their best interest. Did someone rob a bank? The robber likely believed ahead of time that he "should" rob the bank because the chance of getting money was worth the risk of getting caught. What he preferred was *his choice*, even if I preferred otherwise. People tend to do what they think is best for them, whether you think they "must" or "should" do otherwise.

Put a Check on the Projection Bias

Expectations for reciprocity and ideas about how others should behave are an example of what psychologists call the *projection bias*. Each of us has attitudes, beliefs, and priorities that shape how we judge ourselves and others. "Projecting" means assuming that someone else shares your values or beliefs and therefore *should* act accordingly. If just now you were quick to think the equivalent of "No, I am not naïve, I know that people think differently," then pause and consider that you might not be digging deep enough. If you truly did not believe others shared much of your world-view or values, then you would never be surprised or disappointed because you would have no expectations for good behavior. Consider the following statements:

"If I treat others with trust and respect, they will trust and respect me."
"Deep down inside, others value family, truth, health, love (or fill in the blank) as much as I do."

Most of us would agree with these statements, but most of us are wrong. Unless you are a mind-reader or fortune-teller you cannot know with certainty whether someone will reciprocate trust, respect, or whether they share your values. Do not assume what other people are thinking without getting the facts. Generally speaking, whatever someone tells another are mere words until backed up by evidence. Perhaps you would always work toward repaying someone a favor; perhaps you feel gratitude when someone does something good for you; perhaps you occasionally give, expecting nothing in return. But others do not necessarily share your intentions or expectations.

The Selfish Also Make False Assumptions

If you are a person of integrity, dispense with the idea that most other people think like you do. With important exceptions, it is better to believe that many people do not necessarily share your values, even if they are related to you, attend your church or social groups, or even in cases where someone has always seemed to be a close and reliable friend. Selfish individuals project their values onto others, believing that "deep down inside" people are just as selfish as them. In fact, it is dangerous to assume that other people in general think like you do. Not everyone wants social harmony, desires the truth, or places a high value on loyalty, mutual respect, and fairness. For others, these qualities are not as desirable as selfish interests, the desire to dominate others, win at almost all costs, and self-glorification. Whenever you project onto others your own desires, values, attitudes, fears and loves, you put yourself at risk of getting manipulated by those who outwardly appear to share your values, but internally care much more about their own needs and wants than you do as a person.

Use Responsive Rules to Obstruct Difficult People

Letting go of false expectations about difficult people is an accomplishment. The next step is to create psychological and material boundaries. This is accomplished in the following manner:

- Assertively describe the behaviors that you will no longer tolerate.
- Tell the person how you will respond *every time* they engage in the behavior. For example, "If you yell and direct profanities toward me, I will walk away or hang up the phone every time."
- Do not ask or negotiate. You cannot control the other person. Announce how you will respond.
- Be consistent in following through over time.
- Expect that at first the other person will escalate problematic behavior to see if you let things go back to the way they were before you established boundaries.
- Over time, the other person will learn that if they want this or that from you, they need to change their behavior.

Self-Interest Can Trump Merit

Another misconception that comes from projection is the belief that other people respect and reward merit. While "merit" means many things, it basically boils down to a good-faith effort plus a positive outcome. As an example, if an experienced teacher works hard and the students excel in learning, then the teacher's work has merit—perhaps some more than others. Many people value merit and believe some version of the statement, "If I work hard and succeed in my efforts, I will be promoted, valued, respected, or rewarded in some way." However, many people value other things much more than merit, but seldom admit it. Therefore, it is not wise to always assume that people who say they value merit will prioritize it above other, competing interests. For many, selfishness or hidden agendas are much more important than fairness. If promoting a person of merit means a raise, maybe someone less costly will be promoted instead. Perhaps someone wants to promote a friend, but not because they have earned it. There are many possible reasons that those with merit who *should* get promoted do not. *Do not solely rely upon merit to achieve your goals.* In situations when your merit is already known to others and you are not rewarded, it is nearly always better to add an appeal to someone's self-interest in order to achieve your goals.

Persuade by Tapping into the Power of Self-Interest

Individuals are primarily motivated by their own self-interests. Motivate others by identifying and appealing to their self-interests. Convince them that their self-interests are connected to your self-interest. One way to accomplish this effort is to recognize that people are influenced by positive things, such as making money or getting praise, but dislike unpleasant things, such as fear of losing money or esteem from others. Make the case that their ability to get what they want in some specific way is partly based upon your success. For example, "Your bonus depends upon my department's numbers. If I get promoted, I will make it a priority to increase those numbers." Persuasion works best when someone believes that they get something they want and avoid something they do not want.

The Deeper the Self-Interest, the More Compelling

Every one of us has motivations that we are willing to talk about with others, for example, *"I want to get elected Mayor to serve the community."* It is easy to talk about socially acceptable motives, but virtually every person has motivations that are linked to deeper, unspoken desires arising from our emotional and psychological needs. We tend to keep some personal motivations to ourselves, or perhaps share them with a few trusted others. As human beings we have an inborn desire to maintain a positive self-image, so it is common for people to work hard to conceal socially unacceptable motivations. Consider that there are three levels of surface and concealed motivations:

1) Openly disclosed motivations: serving others; pursuing personal or professional growth; pursuing excellence; supporting one's family; gaining knowledge; engaging in creativity or innovation; expressing gratitude; being practical; using one's talents; reciprocating affection; experiencing freedom; making a living.

2) Motives that people reluctantly call to the attention of others: the desire to make more money; gain popularity (friends, social connections); receive positive regard from others (respect, praise); avoid loneliness; possess greater power or authority; appease a demanding person; buy nice things for oneself; make life easier for oneself (but not others); avoid responsibility.

3) Motivations that are not prosocial and are therefore concealed: to control others; display superiority; compensate for low self-esteem; punish someone; engage in vices; seduce others; avoid fears of rejection or embarrassment; make others envious; exercise biased preferences; satisfy sensual appetites (food, sex); execute revenge; impress others.

Notice how these motivations are different; they can be characterized as social, emotional, material, psychological, or situational. Most people have a combination of level 1 and 2 motivations with a small component of level 3 emotions. Selfish individuals are much more likely to be heavily influenced by dysfunctional level 3 motivations in addition to level 1 and 2 motivations. It is not always possible to determine someone else's level 2 or 3 motivations, but if you can, you will find that you possess special, helpful knowledge about a person's self-interests that you might find useful. You may be able to predict their behavior and tap into their self-interests to get your own needs met.

Learn about the Self-Interests of Others

The first step to solving any problem or making a difficult decision is to obtain information. Learn about situational facts, history, and self-interests of others. Try to imagine their point of view, even if you would not approve of it. When it comes to determining self-interests and how to link them to your own needs, use the following guidelines.

- Identify self-interest by noting what motivates someone. If it is not obvious, clues include determining what that person talks about most, how their facial expressions change when they discuss certain topics, what fears they express, and how they react to situations.
- Help the person understand that by acting in a certain way that is to your benefit they are much more likely to get what they want or need than if they do not.
- When appealing to the self-interest of others, assume that short-term desires are usually more powerful than long-term goals. Do not count on long-term goals as high motivators, e.g. "If you fund my project, two years from now both of us will get promoted."

Influence versus Manipulation

Is the appeal to self-interest a form of manipulation? With the right intentions, appealing to self-interest is not manipulation. It is, rather, an attempt to influence someone to obtain a positive outcome. Think of your words and actions as tools to help you accomplish things in life. A hammer can be used as a weapon or not, depending upon someone's intentions. Our knowledge, resources, words, and actions are tools to help us succeed. People of integrity should succeed, and when they do, the world becomes a better place. Steering the actions of another person to achieve a particular goal maximizes the individual and social good. Do not be passive when others are headed in the wrong direction.

You are not a manipulative person unless you: a) have harmful intentions, b) exploit any vulnerability (for example, naïveté), or c) pursue your efforts ruthlessly and without concern for harming others. A manipulator conceals his or her true motivations because they are not socially praiseworthy. Attempting to influence the behavior of others by tapping into their self-interest is not manipulation when there is the absence of these underlying antisocial approaches.

Appeal to Self-Interest, Not Mercy, Even When You Suffer

When we are in pain and suffer, we want someone to care. At the very least we want understanding; better yet, we hope that others will act to help us solve a problem, alleviate our distress, or at least cut us some slack. If your supervisor at work knows how much stress you are under, *maybe* you will be cut some slack, but in many relationships and work environments this expectation is too high. It is totally outside of your control whether someone actually cares about your suffering, or whether, if someone cares, it will be followed by caring actions. You should not go through life automatically expecting: a) that people will care about your suffering and b) if they do care, that they will do something about it. *As a general rule, people care more about how your actions impact them, and less about your suffering.*

Do Not Appeal to Morality

Morality tends to be a weak motivator for behavior when it has to compete with other motivations. A stressful conflict arises when the moral thing to do competes with others' self-interests. This conflict usually occurs under one of two conditions: a) when a moral action is incompatible with something desirable, e.g. *Jeff was told he would get a promotion if he lied about the corporate scandal* or b) when a moral action could result in loss or suffering, e.g. *Jeff was told he would get fired if he did not lie about the corporate scandal.*

There are times when someone has to choose between self-interest and doing the right thing. This dilemma results in conflict between something we desire and our personal values. Our subconscious defense mechanisms then kick in and the mind begins to generate all kinds of "reasons" to justify doing the wrong thing. It is safe to assume that the greater the temptation, the greater the likelihood that someone will prefer self-interest. For this reason it is best not to appeal to someone's sense of morality. If you do, and they act to the contrary, you are likely to be resented for your awareness that there are cracks in the other person's moral self-image, e.g. "I told Jeff it would be deceptive if he pretended not to know about the cooked-up accounting numbers, but instead he lied. Now I have to work with him every day and he resents me."

Taking Inventory

You have only read the first chapter in this book, but think about the observations about selfishness that you have read about. Think about your own psychology, life experiences, and the people you interact with on a regular basis. Find out what needs to be changed to help you achieve your goals.

Ask yourself…

- Do you assume that other people share your values?
- Do you feel blindsided or confused when someone acts selfishly or vindictively?
- Have you treated others with respect only to get treated like garbage in return?
- Are you extremely disappointed when people you thought you could trust end up acting contrary to your will and

best interests?

- Can you identify the problem person in your life at this time? Is it a co-worker, "friend," family member, or someone else?
- What selfish desire or behavior seems more important to this person than you?
- What motivates this person?
- Have you attempted to communicate your concerns with them?
- Can you tolerate some of their annoying behaviors or is it time to confront the issue(s)?
- If you must interact with this person, but find it difficult, what is your strategy for social engagement?

Change Something

Do things differently...

- Stop assuming others share your beliefs about "give and take" in relationships.
- Decide that you are not going to be a punching-bag for selfish people.
- Stop expecting selfish people to change.
- Stop avoiding problems and problem people. Engage with optimal outcomes.

Develop Wisdom

Think about new strategies...

- Be rational and try to see the situation objectively.
- Honor your emotions; in fact, building resentment can be a red flag that something is not right in your relationship.
- Learn to be assertive.
- End relationships with chronically selfish people.
- When you cannot end a relationship with a selfish person,

implement "rules" about how you will interact with them.
- Develop strategies ahead of time to concretely defend yourself from selfish attacks.
- Be consistent in upholding those rules.

Chapter 2

Law 2: You Cannot Win Over the Unwinnable

Say to yourself early in the morning: I shall meet today inquisitive, ungrateful, violent, treacherous, envious, uncharitable men. All these things have come upon them through ignorance of real good and ill. But I, because I have seen that the nature of good is the right, and of ill the wrong...can neither be harmed by any of them, for no man will involve me in wrong, nor can I be angry with my kinsman or hate him; for we have come into the world to work together...
—Marcus Aurelius

The greater the prize, the greater the exposure to greed, envy, deceit, and seduction. The "prize" is whatever you, plus someone else, intensely desires and pursues. Those selfishly willing to achieve at all costs are sometimes rewarded with success—nearly always to the peril of others. It is necessary to engage such personalities strategically; if not, their machinations have the potential to undermine and spoil every effort. A combination of selfishness, intelligence, and ambition is especially dangerous. Some will not stop until they crush the very reputations, spirits, and livelihoods of those who get in their way. Clever and shrewd, they may do so while appearing blameless and even praiseworthy. It is wise to anticipate these possibilities with a plan to respond effectively.

Many individuals of the above description possess abnormally challenging dispositions. We refer to these as *antagonistic personalities* (the entire person is not necessarily the problem, but rather certain aspects of a person, hence "personalities," not "persons"). Examples of such personalities include the controlling, narcissistic, and passive-aggressive. What makes them "unwinnable" is that they are unpredictable, selectively exhibit hostility, and are virtually incapable of change. They can act temporarily irrational and do not respond to typical prosocial tactics. In many environments, they can neither be avoided nor negotiated with in good faith. *Do not respond to such individuals by working hard to win them over; doing so rewards their behavior, gives them power, and consumes your energy.* The harder you work for the approval of an antagonistic personality, the more they will perceive themselves as dominant while you are perceived as submissive. Do not let selfish, ruthless, or manipulative people determine your fate. Do not expect the unmerciful to show mercy.

Clearly many antagonistic personalities are too disturbed to be successful. The focus here is upon those who—despite their undesirable traits—also have qualities that allow them to be rewarded, or at least tolerated, by others. Many have admirable qualities such as self-discipline, charisma, adaptability, and persistence. Many are knowledgeable, intelligent, and possess important skills. They are often capable of concealing their dysfunction around people in power or authority. Some will cleverly target one individual at a time with hostility while maintaining a positive image around others. For these reasons, they are often liked and valued within organizations and inter-personal relationships.

The Antagonistic Thrive When Able to Produce Results

In general, successful outcomes carry more weight than ruthless tactics. This is what allows selfish individuals with antagonistic personalities to survive and thrive: they are tolerated as long as they produce good results. In many organizations, the human factor is trivial compared to things like revenues, efficiencies, and public relations. Never mind that there are stories about intimi-dation tactics. Never mind that an employee with cancer was unjustly fired to avoid higher insurance costs. Those in leadership positions are likely to look the other way if the numbers are impressive and not too many complaints rise to their level. *Success is like gold: it is valued regardless of any method used to get it.* With some exceptions, people are much more impressed by successful outcomes than the means used to obtain those outcomes. On an individual level this means that methods to get what one wants are less important than self-gratification.

An antagonistic supervisor or co-worker who targets another person can cause a great deal of misery. Usually the motive is personal gain of some kind, but not always. An individual can be targeted due to envy, vindictiveness, greed, or by those who simply enjoy dominating or tormenting others whenever they can get away with it. Because these personalities interact with others atypically, ordinary methods to solve problems and resolve conflicts tend to fail.

A similar phenomenon also occurs in personal relationships. Antagonistic personalities have relationships and get married just like everyone else. They tend to mask their true character to please a partner, but over time, attempts to dominate or manipulate the other person result in conflict that can be destructive to others, including children. Under such circumstances, it is easy to feel powerless as the other person does not change, despite negotiating, pleading, and arguing. This pattern typically results in depression, anger, and can even take a toll on one's physical health. Adults who grew up in dysfunctional or abusive families might find themselves reliving a slightly different version of a familiar nightmare.

Antagonistic Personality Types

The controlling

Rigid and perfectionistic, controlling personalities attempt to dominate others. They are prone to excessive anger when their draconian standards are not met.

The hyper-critical

Hyper-critical people are excessively judgmental. They have opinions about everything and are good at arguing. They display condescending criticisms toward others with an air of superiority. They think in an all-or-nothing manner, e.g. "I'm right and you're wrong."

The pretentious

These individuals make a good show of saying what you want to hear without any intention of following through. They appear to be sympathetic, but quickly become disloyal when it is to their advantage.

The passive-aggressive

Passive-aggressive individuals are resentful, but do not openly express their resentments in order to avoid conflict or negative consequences. Instead, they work behind the scenes to undermine others, using such tactics as procrastination, gossiping, intentional inefficiency, and complaining.

The narcissistic

Narcissists believe they are superior to others and are therefore entitled to praise, favors, and special treatment. They can be arrogant, grandiose, charismatic, and capable of impressing others (especially at first). Like one-dimensional characters, these traits are superficial facades that fall apart under scrutiny. Incapable of empathy, they pursue their own needs, even if it involves deception, manipulation, or actively harming others (usually emotionally and psychologically).

The sadistic

Sadists get pleasure from the suffering of others. They tend to use whatever power they have to frustrate others. It is common for them to promise favors or money, only to string someone along as long as possible. They usually get involved with projects only to interfere with success, resulting in misery.

The psychopathic

Psychopaths do not have a moral compass and use deception, seduction, and charm to manipulate their victims. If these approaches do not work, they can become intimidating or even aggressive. They do not experience remorse, but are aware of the emotions of others, which they will opportunistically exploit.

The dramatic

A mess of contradictions, dramatic individuals vacillate between extremes. A calm mood can suddenly turn into a bout of sad tearfulness or explosive anger. Because they are prone to misinterpreting the actions of others, their expressions of trust and affection can be followed by accusations at the slightest provocation. Some need to be the center of attention, even when it is inappropriate to the situation. When distressed, they are typically not responsive to rational explanations.

Special Considerations

Not all antagonistic types are capable of being ruthless. For example, unlike psychopaths, most hyper-critical people are capable of empathy and remorse. Many have more than one trait without a dominant theme emerging. For example, some of the traits shared by controlling people are also shared by the hyper-critical. Do not write these individuals off as mentally sick. Many antagonistic types are highly successful and have no history of psychiatric illness. Focus upon responding in a productive way, not diagnosing people.

Note that the vast majority of us, under the right circumstances, can *temporarily* share some of the traits described above.

In Chapter 1 we referred to the "weakly virtuous" as basically normal people who become prone to negative behavior under certain circumstances. As levels of stress, fear, and social pressure increase, our animal instincts to survive take over while our higher brain functions, responsible for empathy and logical thinking, get sidelined. But when these strains go away, normal morality returns, and we act according to our values. Thus someone who is ordinarily "a little critical," under stress, might temporarily become very critical. This kind of experience is normal and to be expected under certain conditions.

What Makes Us Vulnerable?

We get blindsided

Most of us are not used to dealing with toxic personalities. Seemingly out of nowhere a personal attack throws us off balance. We hope it is a fluke, only for a pattern to emerge, but by then damage has already been done.

We falsely believe that with the right approach, things can be worked out

Prosocial tactics like direct communication, rational dialogue, and a willingness to compromise sometimes prove effective with antagonistic personalities, but only when they are linked to self-interest in the mind of the antagonistic personality; otherwise, they are at best superficial interactions, and at worst, completely useless.

We incorrectly assume some version of the statements:

"If I am a positive, friendly person, this person will grow to like me."

Or

"This person will leave me alone if I am not perceived as a threat or competitor."

We like to believe that deep down inside, every person wants to get along with others, so we come up with excuses for difficult people, e.g. "They're just defensive, scared, or sensitive." But antagonistic personalities are selfish regardless of the kindness, acceptance, and supportiveness of others. They are selfish even when they appear to be unselfish. They do not care about whether you are harmless; in fact, this is likely to be interpreted as weakness and submissiveness, thereby increasing the odds that you will become a target. Always remember that antagonistic personalities cannot be won over by persistent niceness, which is the equivalent of offering flowers to a venomous snake. If you try to win them over, you will likely be perceived as a sucker, vulnerable to being taken advantage of by others. If you ever find yourself a target of an antagonistic personality, do not increase your niceness to demonstrate that you are harmless; it will only make your situation worse.

We crave validation and our self-worth is defined by others

Many of us believe (usually unconsciously) that we should be liked for who we are by almost everyone and that not being liked is a problem. But where does this disposition come from? The answer partly lies in our childhoods. Our very identity and sense of self is shaped by our interactions with others—a phenomenon that psychologists call the "looking-glass self." Children know what is praiseworthy or not because of the feedback they get from others. But as we live and learn, things get confusing as we experience a huge discrepancy between real-life experiences and societal ideals. *While our highest ideals assure us that inner beauty is most important, that we should think for ourselves, and that esteem should come from within, the vast majority of us are almost entirely dependent upon others for validation.* As adults we continue to rely on the praise and acceptance others provide us with for validation. No one can deny that it is natural to want others to like and appreciate you, but to mostly depend upon others for validation and esteem gives others a lot of power and makes you a victim of fickle opinion. Society itself reinforces the idea that we are valued because others value us. Human beings are social by nature and we tend to think alike; in the contemporary world this "herd" mentality assures that those who go too far in bucking mainstream opinions risk exclusion from career and relationship opportunities.

We take things personally

It is only natural to experience negative emotions when interacting with antagonistic personalities. Accept the feelings of anger, anxiety, and frustration caused by such individuals. If you try too hard to suppress these feelings, you risk becoming eccentric. *Rooted in the past, the negative aspects of human personality are more complex and bigger than you or anything you can do about it.* Do not attempt to change the mindset of an antagonistic personality; if you try, the result will be frustration and failure. The only healthy response is to change your perspective. In the big picture, nothing about social engagement is personal. In fact, if you take things personally, you will be emotionally unsettled and therefore distracted from achieving your objectives.

First Response: Assess the Power Differential

When dealing with antagonistic personalities, first assess your level of power and authority in relation to the other person. Obviously you cannot use just any approach when someone can cause personal loss. The suggested responses in this chapter must be used gently and cautiously with superiors. Use your best judgment. On the other hand, if you encounter challenging personalities who have less power or authority than you do, then the threat of consequences, such as losing a job or ending a relationship, should carry more weight than any tactic.

An antagonistic personality who is your equal in authority

can be the most frustrating challenger to your success. Those above you may be indifferent to your conflict while others lower on the totem pole have no power or desire to come to your assistance. The very greatest threats to your efforts are individuals who match you in skill, ability, and intelligence. This observation is true in nearly every sphere of human interactions, but most commonly in the political aspects of work and within personal relationships that have deteriorated into entrenched conflict. When your equals are antagonistic personalities, expect them to use escalating tactics to remove you as a perceived obstacle to what they want. Charm and niceness are usually followed by deception or manipulation, which later escalate into accusations, criticisms, and allegations of incompetence. End-game tactics can include intimidation, sabotage, or even aggression. Sometimes the plan is to unsettle your emotional state or undermine your social reputation. For such individuals, "winning" usually means that someone is no longer an obstacle to their object of desire.

Assume Concealed Agendas

It is a good idea to totally avoid, if possible, antagonistic personalities. But avoidance is not always possible or advantageous. The second most successful way to manage antagonistic personalities is the same for anyone else: appealing to their self-interest. A win-win scenario acceptable to both parties could result in a "truce" of sorts. However, this is not always possible because antagonistic personalities often conceal true motivations that are not socially acceptable. A note of caution is warranted: even when you learn what motivations someone might possess, it is not always in your interest to appeal to them. Your reputation will suffer if others discover that you were complicit in appealing to dysfunctional sentiments such as envy, personal vendettas, arrogance, or greed. For the above reasons, other responses are sometimes required.

Convey Self-Respect and Defiance

The ideal mental attitude when dealing with antagonistic personalities is based upon resilient core beliefs. *It is utterly critical to believe—deep in the core of your being—that to be respected is much more important than to be liked.* "Respect" in this sense does not mean being appreciated; it means that you have decided that you will not be driven away, give up, fall apart, or acquiesce in response to personal attacks. It means that you affirm your dignity, which can never be taken away from you. A defiant attitude allows a person to withstand personal attacks, but also makes them less vulnerable. Someone with a sense of self-respect does not present as weak and submissive, hence, they are less likely to be targeted by antagonistic personalities.

To convey the right image, you must avoid subtle, non-verbal signs of submissiveness as well. Do not apologize unless necessary, and when you do apologize, do so succinctly. Do not complain or display emotional weakness. Do not ramble on and on about your woes. Avoid disclosing unnecessary details about your thoughts and plans. In dealing with antagonistic personalities, recognize that you might be in a situation where nothing you do will win them over to your point of view. Adopt a defiant attitude. Everything about you must convey that you are not submissive, even if you have little external control. Defiance is very different from hostility: it does not convey a desire for retaliation or vindictiveness, nor is it aggressive. Defiance means taking a stand against oppressive people, rejecting acquiescence, and affirming your own self-confidence. Realize that your own dignity cannot be taken away from you, but it can be given away, and you must protect it at all costs.

Eliminate What Makes You Vulnerable to Hostility

If you find yourself a target of social marginalization or active persecution from antagonistic personalities (or others) you must first of all objectively assess the situation. Begin by asking yourself whether there is anything about you that makes you vulnerable to social criticism that you are willing to change. You will know that you display vulnerability if you have experienced similar social problems in different environments with different people. To use an example, if a child gets picked on by bullies in one school, perhaps it is bad luck. But if the child changes schools four times and gets bullied each time, then there is probably some unique characteristic that makes the child vulnerable to becoming a target of hostility. Avoid getting caught up in the notion that the bullies are the ones who need to change. This pointless righteous indignation is only a distraction away from solving the real problem. As an adult you have more options than children and should use your skills and intelligence to your advantage. Determine your differences or weaknesses, and if they are a source of criticism from others, you might want to remove them. Often, harmless or subtle differences in behavior or physical appearance are enough to result in someone becoming an object of prey. If you cannot remove them, choose to embrace them, and do so boldly. The absence of shame is a mark of self-respect.

Our sophisticated ideas about how to deal with difficult people are sometimes put to shame by the honesty of children. Consider the false idea, encouraged by well-meaning teachers, that a child can stop bullying by saying "Please stop" or "I feel sad/angry/hurt when you do that to me." When a child informs you that these methods do not work, you should believe the child. If a bigger child takes a smaller child's ball, and the smaller child complains, the smaller child is likely to be told, "Shut up! I don't care. It's my ball now!" All the assertiveness coaching in the world will not amount to a hill of beans difference when dealing with a seasoned bully who simply wants their way. Hostility cannot be overcome by niceness. This is true for adults as well as children.

Use Diplomatic and Psychotherapeutic Tactics

The fields of psychotherapy and diplomacy have several aspects of import to the topic at hand: they address self-interest, strategy, and optimal responses to conflict—the one on an interpersonal level, the other on an international level. Each must convey the impression of objectivity and fairness while simultaneously having an agenda (one hopes, for positive purposes). Many of the methods used by diplomats and psychotherapists can also be used in social situations by anyone with the prerequisite skill and patience. Some methods include: exploiting weaknesses, mirroring, dismissing, imposing responsive rules, saving face, and tapping the imagination.

Exploit the weaknesses of the antagonistic person

Notice when someone else is overcompensating for some weakness. The prideful person doubtless fears being ordinary; the perfectionist fears mistakes; the angry person fears being perceived as someone without self-control. While it is better to overcome weakness by transformation, most find that very difficult and choose the easier path of protecting their egos from injury. They go through life on autopilot, hoping to get by. Most find it very difficult to face and accept their fears and instead take the easier path of building psychological walls to protect their vulnerabilities. The strongest of such individuals successfully safeguard their frailties.

Notice someone else's weakness—not to do them harm but to unsettle them if they attack you. Even if you cannot strike at their core you can unsettle them by making them aware of some menacing threat to the ego. Under higher levels of stress and pressure the ability for self-control becomes fragile and one must work hard to maintain a homeostasis. These times provide the best opportunity to notice the weaknesses of an antagonistic personality.

Is it ethical to exploit the weaknesses of others? Most of the time it is not, but sometimes it is acceptable because you are trying to defend yourself. Remember that you have more noble goals than an antagonistic person; therefore you deserve to succeed more than they do. There is such a thing as *ethical exploitation*. When you use someone else's greed, deception, or selfishness against them for a positive outcome, you are using your knowledge about them for a higher purpose. For example, selfishness is often kept in check by fear of punishment. Many more people would steal from their employers if they thought they could get away with it. When people are reminded they could lose their jobs or go to jail for stealing, their fear is exploited to ensure good behavior. It is no different when you use a selfish person's own weaknesses to achieve a positive goal, defend yourself or minimize harm in some way.

Mirroring Tactics

Validate feelings, not beliefs

As noted earlier, most antagonistic personalities experience little or zero empathy or sympathy for others, but ironically, they usually respond very positively to it themselves. This makes them vulnerable to lowering their guard, especially when they are unhappy. Believing themselves to be victims rather than victimizers, they soak up empathy, kindness, and encouragement from others. They interpret this as agreement with their point of view. They easily jump to conclusions and misinterpret sentiment for their suffering as support for their beliefs. These kinds of responses can serve to temporarily decrease antagonism toward you.

For this approach to be successful and ethical make sure that you empathize or sympathize with the feelings and sufferings of the other person, but without affirming their dysfunctional beliefs. For example, if a narcissist complained, "I'm so angry. I am the most intelligent person here and I deserved a raise! I

41

should be the one running this company!" a reflective response could be, "That sounds tough. If you deserved a raise, but didn't get it, no wonder you're angry." Notice how the reply never asserts that the narcissist actually deserved a raise; rather the *feeling*, anger, was validated under the condition "if" the person actually deserved a raise.

Disarm with reflection

When people talk, they expect others to give advice, criticize, and attempt to turn the focus back upon them. They are surprised when someone is actually a good listener who really tries to understand what has been said in a non-judgmental way. Antagonistic personalities are no different. They crave validation, which feeds their ego. One way to disarm antagonistic personalities is to paraphrase their own words back to them, but slightly altered to avoid parroting. This lets them know that you totally understand and "get" their point of view. For example, if a person stated, "Amy always ignores me! What is her problem? I should dump her," a reply could be, "So you reach out to her and she doesn't respond? No wonder you're considering leaving her."

Reflective questioning can also be helpful. Asking questions never involves directly asserting anything and therefore is not likely to be challenged. But with the right word choice, questioning can feel validating. Someone who says, "That idiot will not pay me back my money!" might feel validated with the response, "Isn't it awful when people are unfair?" This type of communication is non-judgmental and therefore non-confrontational.

Use mimicry

One mistake people make is they think they must counter antagonism by responding differently than the antagonist. But this response is disadvantageous when the antagonistic person has already first acted with the best tactic. In such a circumstance, mimicry can prove effective. When we act like a mirror, mimicking what someone does, we infuriate and frustrate others. This tit-for-tat has the advantage of conveying to others what it is like to be on the receiving end of undesirable behavior. This tactic is intentionally annoying, but ultimately harmless. Besides, if you are dealing with active hostility, desperate times call for desperate measures. As an example, imagine two car companies engaged in competitive advertising. One of the car companies could mimic the advertising scheme of the other company by advertising in the same media outlets for the same amount of time.

On an individual level, mimicry forces a lose-lose scenario for an antagonistic person: if they do not stop their actions, they will experience the same thing they are inflicting upon others. Mimicry also compels a feeling of shame because there are no grounds to complain without seeming ridiculous; after all, they are the ones that first did it to someone else. Of course the hope is that they stop this cycle of madness and adjust their behavior, but if not, they are choosing their own consequences. This tactic also makes you unpredictable—at any time you could stop mimicking and do something else, but no one knows whether or when you will change your approach.

Impose responsive rules

When you become the object of antagonistic tactics, it sometimes proves effective to commit to responding in a specific way every time, e.g. "Every time he does X, I will respond by doing Y." For example, *"Every time Janice ignores my calls, I will ignore her request for more supplies."* In interpersonal relationships this can be effective as well, for example, *"Every time Jim flirts with another woman I will get up and leave, even if I have to take a taxi home."* This tactic is best accomplished by openly declaring your plan. Tell the other person that you will respond in a particular manner to them. If you do not inform the other party of your plan, it will be viewed by third parties as passive-aggressive and dysfunctional. Responsive rules work because the undesirable behavior becomes associated with an undesirable response. This is the equivalent of a young child learning, "Every time I touch the burner it hurts."

It is okay to make variations to your responsive rules, but be consistent. Expect resistance at first as the antagonistic person tests your resolve. If you quit, the same tactic will not work as well the second time. But with consistency the other person will learn that "If I do X, I will get Y in return. If I do not want Y, I need to stop doing X."

Give them what they want to their own peril

Once upon a time it was common for parents to punish children for smoking by forcing them to smoke to the point of sickness. It was believed that such a negative experience would stop a child from wanting to smoke. Many adults, like children, desire things that are not good for them. When we help (or do not hinder) a selfish person's efforts to get what they want, it is they, not we, who bear the responsibility for their suffering—they asked for it as mature adults. If an antagonistic person desires something that is self-defeating, then let them have that experience. This approach is sometimes used in political engagement. For example, it is common for a novice political underdog to try to gain traction by goading a more experienced opponent to debate in town hall meetings. When the opponent gives in to the demand, the underdog ends up doing poorly—having gotten what was demanded, but only to a disadvantage.

Dismiss with humor or contempt

Eventually someone is likely to approach you with unreasonable demands and opinions, presented with an air of seriousness. If you waste your energy responding with rational objections, you bring credibility to the other person's point of view because you too are taking it seriously. Instead, show contempt or humor for their ideas with dismissive statements like, "That's ridiculous," or "Are you trying to drive me crazy?" or (laughing) "Good one. Please tell me you're not serious!" This lets others know that it is time to move along to other things because you do not want to waste your time. This is effective because usually the other person knows (but will not admit) that his or her ideas are not credible enough to be taken seriously.

Tap into the imagination

When people get stuck in little conflicts they lose sight of the big picture. A battle over a detail can become emotional and people forget about larger goals. When this happens, remind them not to lose sight of the larger objective. Someone is much more likely to compromise on small issues if they believe it is their best chance to win later on larger issues. This method works best when two parties share the same larger goal. For example, in warfare, two enemies might ally to engage a common enemy (like the United States and the Soviet Union did against the Nazis in World War II). But any two individuals, teams, or organizations can choose to look past their differences to achieve a higher end-goal. Social psychologists call these kinds of goals "superordinate."

Give someone an out, e.g. "saving face"

As you become more strategic in social engagement, you will frequently best those who oppose you. This can be dangerous because the wounded pride of those who opposed you is likely to produce resentments that build up over time. To decrease the odds of this happening, give someone a graceful way to back out of a conflict or take a loss. More than likely, the other person will understand that you allowed this to happen, helping to decrease ill will and keep the relationship at least civil. Even an antagonistic personality—if the ego is not too wounded—is less likely to be vindictive when they save face.

Work to totally remove hostile individuals

Highly antagonistic and hostile individuals do not believe in reciprocity. It is therefore foolish to think, as many good people do, some version of, "People will appreciate it when I do not return evil for evil." Sure, some people will appreciate it, but antagonistic individuals will misinterpret your magnanimity as an attempt to gloat or appear morally superior. Do not make the mistake of being kind to a poisonous snake; your kindness will be despised and you will get bitten. It is better for you (and probably for others) that you boldly, not timidly, remove the other person from their ability to associate with you or retaliate against you. Do whatever it legally takes to make this happen—firing them, getting a no-contact order from a court, forcing an eviction, excommunicating them from a social group, etc.

Practice indifference with the unremittingly hostile

The authors of this book hesitated to add this section because the main idea can be misunderstood and misused. It is also hard to implement. But the following tactic is necessary for those of us forced by circumstances to associate with extremely hostile and antagonistic individuals. This tactic is appropriately applied by individuals who believe that keeping their job, social group, or family intact is very important, regardless of the fact that it entails interacting with an extremely difficult individual. Note: the following tactic should not be used in collapsing romantic relationships.

There are (hopefully) very few times in life when you encounter someone you cannot avoid that is extremely and unremittingly antagonistic or hostile. When this unfortunate circumstance arises and you have exhausted all other options there is little left to do but become completely indifferent to their thoughts, feelings, and behaviors. In essence, you actively: a) cease having any hope of getting along with them in the future, b) cease communicating with them unless absolutely necessary, and c) become completely indifferent toward them in every way. This is a very difficult tactic to implement because it involves turning off your emotions—both negative and positive—and letting go of any expectations at all for future reconciliation.

To be successful with this tactic you must communicate with the other person *only* when utterly necessary, accompanied by brevity of speech and an expressionless face. Any negativity is met with silence or indifference as the only allowed topics are facts and necessities. Think of "Spock" on *Star Trek*. This tactic can be incredibly effective. It is a form of shunning that marginalizes the other person away from you and neutralizes their offensiveness. It is usually maddening for your opponent when his or her arrows no longer cause you pain. Be aware that initially your opponent will escalate the problematic behaviors to see if you crack, but if you are consistent, over time there will be less and less energy expended to oppress you. More than likely, this individual will eventually find someone else to torment. Do not be deceived with any attempts to woo you back; if you do, you will regret it and this approach will not work a second time. This tactic requires commitment and needs to be long-term to be effective. It is crucial that you be utterly consistent in using this strategy and that it only applies to the person in question—not associates or even friends of your opponent. Do not use this strategy with your superiors or anyone who has power over you. Before you begin, assess whether the other person could someday be in a position where they have power or authority over you.

Perhaps you are wondering how this strategy is ethical in the first place. After all, anyone can change, and maybe you should not become indifferent to another human being. However, shunning someone does not require that you actually believe that someone is personally hopeless or worthless. It is more analogous to what society does to serious criminals: extreme marginalization for the protection of society. Just because someone has a life sentence in prison does not mean they would reoffend, it just means they have acted so destructively that society cannot take that chance. In a similar way, the focus of this tactic should be someone who has repeatedly acted in such a hostile manner that you have let go of any positive expectations for them whatsoever for your own protection. You should not hate them, which will disturb your mind, but you should act completely indifferent toward them.

Specific Tactics According to Subtype

The above were general tactics. Now let us proceed to tactics specific to different types of antagonistic personalities. Note that due to similarities among types, some are grouped together.

Responding to the Controlling and Hyper-Critical

What the hyper-critical and controlling have in common is that they value their assumptions very highly and view others as inferior. You are "wrong" if you disagree with them. Your feelings, personal experiences, and motivations are of little importance to such individuals, who typically respond with coldness and condescension. Rather than merely stating the facts, they pass on their own opinions about things as if they were facts. In reality, their judgments are personal ideas of right and wrong from a narrow point of view. They falsely assume or exaggerate their ability to read others' backgrounds, personal-ities, and motivations based on their own assumptions. They act like they always know what is best. They usually categorize people based on superficial impressions without getting to know someone's true character or inner motivations. They quickly notice and give undue weight to how someone looks or acts, with special attention paid to obvious flaws in physical appearance and interpersonal style. Sympathy is seldom given.

One way to know if you are dealing with a controlling or hyper-critical personality is to ask yourself whether you feel "graded" poorly about yourself or something you did. These individuals frequently make other people feel demoralized and totally incompetent. This is exactly what they want because they are eager to fill the void left when others lose confidence so they can have more power to control things and make decisions. If you give in to their criticisms, you will feel yourself getting smaller and smaller over time.

There are three key weaknesses of both types. First, they tend to make assumptions prior to getting all the information they need to make a conclusion. They avoid directly asking questions, which they view as a position of weakness. Second, they make social errors by conveying contempt or irritability toward others. Third, they often make faulty generalizations about people based upon deviations from what is "normal." For example, a hyper-critical personality might believe that if a person is poor, then they must be lazy. Even if that is true some of the time, it does not mean that the next poor person you encounter is lazy. But generalizations are sometimes accurate, thus it might seem like this kind of person is frequently "right" in their opinion; however, when they get it wrong, it is at the expense of justice because individuals are unique. They tend to not be compassionate because they devalue intangibles such as emotions, personal problems, and bad luck. Did Jose arrive late? Well, he should have gotten up early and read the traffic report. Did Julie cry during a meeting because she couldn't keep it together after her mother died? Then she should have stayed home. The controlling and hyper-critical are rarely kind.

Tactics

Assess whether the person is correct

The hyper-critical and controlling are not idiots; in fact, they tend to be of above average intelligence. Even if you do not like such persons, if you know they are correct, swallow your pride and admit it.

Avoid arguing

Arguing is the turf of controlling and hyper-critical personalities. You are at a disadvantage if you engage them in argument. They believe their judgments are superior to those of others, thus, even if you "win" an argument, it will be an empty victory; they are not likely to change their minds and the subsequent resentment could lead to retaliation.

Reframe the opinion without the judgmental language

These types of antagonistic personalities try to give credibility to their judgmental attitudes by mixing facts with opinions. Consider the following critical statement: "There were many design flaws because the designer is an idiot!" Like the industrious ant, respond by taking the sugar, but leaving the dirt behind. A proper reply might be, "You're right about the fact there were many design flaws, but I want to know how to fix the problem." This kind of response does not challenge the other person, thereby avoiding conflict, nor does it require you to agree with a judgmental statement.

Do not necessarily take them seriously

Excessive judgmental attitudes and perfectionism have little credibility because they are rigid extremes. Do not take seriously frequently given strong opinions based on a narrow point of view. Let them babble, but focus on other things that are not a waste of your time.

Discern the underlying message and call them on it

Beneath every criticism is a veiled message that usually breaks down into some variation of the notions, "I am better than you" or "I think that person is inferior." When you speak out loud the hidden message, especially around others, you force either a shameful admission or a retraction. For example, "You've repeatedly implied that Sarah makes bad decisions. Do you think she's stupid? Do you think you can do better than her?"

Identify and push emotional buttons

Judgmental and critical antagonistic types usually take pride in their intellect and want others to think they possess self-control. However, since the world seldom conforms to their standards, anger or irritability always lies just beneath the surface. It is highly annoying to them when you focus upon their emotions. Use open-ended questions to provoke them, e.g. "Are you angry about that? Are you sure?" Call attention to non-verbal behaviors, e.g. "You seem a little tense. Are you sure you're not pissed off?"

Question definitions

Hyper-critical and controlling individuals tend to express *subjective opinions* rather than *objective descriptions*. Rather than merely describing a fact, like, "Tim was late to the meeting," they add their own opinions, e.g. "Tim is always late because he can't get his act together." The latter part of the sentence, "…because he can't get his act together," is hardly a fact and falls apart under scrutiny. Is he really "always" late? How do you define his "act"? Let others get stuck in the quicksand of trying to define their own explanations. But if you stick with describing the facts and let others pass judgment, over time you will notice that your wisdom surpasses their wit. You are also less likely to be viewed as contentious. Skepticism is safer, more logical, and immune to error because it only describes—it does not assert.

There are of course times when you need to voice opinions. Do so cautiously and let your actions speak louder than words. In the above example about "Tim" a manager could later say, "We value our meetings. I've just emailed out our policy for meeting attendance standards." Enough said. People will learn your opinion by witnessing your actions. Why put opinions on "the record" when actions are more powerful?

Responding to the Pretentious and Passive-Aggressive

The pretentious and passive-aggressive have something in common: they present to others a positive image while using indirect methods to exercise hostility. The pretentious use insincere compliments, feigned interest, and convincing words to convey the impression of support, only to later betray you when it is to their advantage. Passive-aggressive individuals are resentful, but avoid open confrontation and undermine others with "passive" actions such as procrastination, gossiping, intentional inefficiency, and subtle criticism.

But let us look at the big picture. To a milder degree, the vast majority of us are a little passive-aggressive and pretentious. We choose—sometimes from affection, but often from necessity—to appear agreeable to avoid offending others. Society usually rewards the agreeable, positive person, even if that person is inauthentic. Pretentious people just take it to another level. Similarly, most of us are a little passive-aggressive from time to time because society provides us with few socially acceptable outlets for aggression. We have to appear calm and prosocial regardless of provocations. Did the CEO do something infuriating? Keep quiet and smile at the next meeting. Did my wife just insult me? I can't blow up in front of the kids. We also have more laws, regulations, monitoring, and standards for etiquette than ever before in human history. Political correctness—with all of its pros and cons—means we have to speak carefully or get into trouble. To avoid conflict and consequences a lot of us walk around constantly censoring our words and suppressing our feelings.

For some, however, passive-aggression and pretentiousness are defining characteristics. It is their "normal." Combined with hostility, they become destructive. Usually intelligent, these individuals target others in subtle yet unsettling ways. Their words and actions are disguised so well that they can later deny any knowledge or responsibility for negativity. Some will harm others while claiming good intentions, e.g. "I'm not harassing you, dear. I left you 23 messages because I was concerned about you." Some are superficially nice, but mix their criticisms with little "digs" that make others feel insecure, e.g. "Annie, your programming is excellent. That reminds me, the best programming in this department has been done by Sasha. I'm going to go tell her that right now."

Tactics

Nail them down by insisting upon specifics

Vague language is the friend of the passive-aggressive or pretentious person, e.g. "I will do it." "You can count on me." Later, time goes by and nothing has changed. Do not settle for nonspecifics. Insist upon dates, times, and commitments, e.g. "You agreed to do it, now name a day and time when it will be done." The more specific the commitment, the harder it is for someone to get away with procrastination or intentional delay tactics.

Call them on it

What the pretentious fear most is disapproval of others. In their attempts to avoid disapproval they agree with everyone, but commit to nothing. Eventually, they make the mistake of agreeing with two or more people who have contrary opinions. To force their hand, find another person who has an entirely different opinion from yours and insist that the suspected pretentious person give their opinion, e.g. "Both of us are here with you right now, Jack. Tell us which one of our ideas you think is best." This is a lose-lose scenario for them: either they disagree with one party or are exposed as noncommittal people-pleasers.

A version of this is applicable to the passive-aggressive. They have learned that open displays of hostility result in social disapproval, so they hide their true feelings. Unsettle them by calling attention to their true feelings. Speak out loud in a questioning, non-accusatory manner about their negativity. For example, "Do you hate your job?" "Do you feel resentful about things around here?" "Are you jealous of me?" etc. When they deny these feelings you can up the ante with follow-up questions, e.g. "So you don't hate your job? Great, then tell me the things you like about it?"

Ignore, but do not reinforce complaining

People who complain about you can undermine your efforts. On the other hand, complaints you hear from other people are attempts to get you to sympathize or justify their unhappiness. When "normal" people complain, it might be fine to commiserate a little bit, but it is best to ignore chronic complainers. If needed, jump beyond their complaints by only responding to the factual part of what was said. If a complainer says, "We work hard around here and get no respect," acknowledge the factual part, "We work hard around here," but do not contribute to the part, "…and we get no respect."

Be annoyingly positive

Passive-aggressive people are negative and resentful. If you are positive, encouraging, and point out good things, they are likely to respond by avoiding you. For example, if one professor said to the other, "The students these days are almost as stupid as our administration," a positive response could be, "My experience has been that many of our students are fast learners. And our administrators really seem to care and be working hard to keep enrollment up." This type of invalidation is infuriating to the passive-aggressive, who seek out others to confirm their misery.

Pay attention to actions, but be wary of flowery language

The pretentious are skilled flatterers. Be skeptical if someone says all of the right things all of the time. Wait until they are required to act on those sentiments before you become a believer. Do not be content with symbolic gestures. The greater the effort or sacrifice, the less likely it is that they are pretentious.

Responding to the Narcissistic, Psychopathic, and Sadistic

These antagonistic personalities are similar because they are extremely selfish and lack empathy. They rarely, if ever, feel remorse for the emotional and psychological pain they inflict upon others. They can perform well at school or work when they possess the ability to control their impulses and delay gratification. Eventually some become successful in society by presenting an acceptable public image and outwardly playing by the rules most of the time. When they get their way, all is well; when they do not, they will use any means at their disposal to fulfill their needs, unless deterred by fear of consequences.

They tend to target specific victims who are weak, powerless, or vulnerable while maintaining cordial or friendly relations with others. Some possess an underlying need to assert their superiority by dominating or humiliating others. Persistent virtue is considered foolish, childlike, and unconvincing. Human beings are viewed as objects and a means to an end. Their victims typically experience negative emotions and psychological distress. There is usually a history of many failed relationships; enduring relationships are often had with a partner who enables their dysfunction.

For most, there is an absence of accurate reflection upon their own selfish motives and intentions. To avoid negative self-reflection, they develop a positive self-image. Beneath this self-image lie entirely selfish motives, desires, and intentions. They believe they are good; in fact, better than others. Due to this self-deception, they usually believe that they are the victims and will portray themselves as such quite easily, even when they are the perpetrators of harm, e.g. "You made me spread rumors about you because you wouldn't listen to me." They will not hesitate to lie, and then deny or excuse the lie when confronted. Seeing nothing wrong with themselves, they are the least likely of any subtype to change in any significant way.

Tactics

Do not appear weak

Lions stalk the weak and wounded. The greatest protection for you is to appear strong, self-confident, and unwilling to acquiesce to personal attacks. If you struggle with self-esteem and timidity, you might have to "fake it until you make it." Do not become accommodating or generous without good reason. Having strong friends and associates is also helpful. Do not meet with them one-on-one unless necessary. Having others around as witnesses will deter antisocial behavior. When they notice that you are not an easy target, they will move on to someone else.

Increase transparency

These antagonistic types frequently present a positive image as camouflage to conceal their unscrupulous methods. This works because people falsely associate qualities like charm, attractiveness, intelligence, and likeability as indications of morality.

Psychologists refer to this tendency as the *attributional bias*. But like a light in the darkness, transparency exposes deceptive and ruthless tactics. Examples of transparency include requiring a high level of accountability, open and honest communication, and a work culture of sharing resources and information.

Manipulate the timing, frequency, and duration of interactions

There may be times when you may not have the authority or power to compel someone to cease hostile behavior. In response, you can either passively hope it stops on its own, or you can take control of ancillary variables to influence the order and structure of the relationship. By setting ground rules for interaction you can channel the course of behavior by insisting upon a set of prerequisite conditions. *This is best accomplished by manipulating the variables of time, frequency, and duration of human communication in order to increase predictability and control.* These efforts are helpful because you are essentially imposing "rules" on others, who will be frustrated in their attempts to surprise you or take advantage of you. For example, "My mother-in-law hates me, but I must see her. I will only see her once a month for no more than 45 minutes per visit." Antagonistic personalities will not like your "rules," but if they want access to you by communicating or associating with you, there is little they can do but submit to your structure. There are several ways this can be accomplished.

If someone can demand your presence at any time, they have power over you: *they* decide when to communicate because you want to avoid them; *they* decide what subject to discuss. Meanwhile, you are left enduring unpleasant company, hoping they will either become reasonable or go away. Regain the upper hand by informing the other person that you will only engage them for a specific amount of time or frequency. Set minimum standards for acceptable behavior. Let them know that these are "rules" you have chosen to live by—do not negotiate or expect them to agree. You should make clear that when someone violates your conditions you will shut down communications completely until they comply.

Responding to the Dramatic

The antagonistically dramatic both allure and repel others. They tend to be personally engaging, uninhibited—even seductive. On the other hand, they are unpredictable and highly reactive. Some create drama and distress and are prone to emotional outbursts; others feel the need to be the center of attention and find anything less boring. Many are too challenged by emotional extremes to be highly successful; others rise to the top due to desirable qualities such as intelligence, skill, creativity, and attractiveness. They are not likely to be a problem for you in a low power position. However, those that have risen high enough in a hierarchy will act out against others, feeling they can do what they want without fear of consequences. It is even more common for a person to develop a personal relationship with a dramatic person, only to find themselves trapped in chaos.

The "red flag" is emotional lack of self-control characterized by bouts of rage, moodiness, irritability, or tearful sadness. However, some have learned to temporarily suppress intense negative emotions when it really counts. Their weaknesses include difficulty tolerating even well-intentioned criticism, which they interpret as a hostile, personal attack, an intolerance of boredom or being alone, and fears of abandonment. They desire constant interactions with others to distract them from chronic feelings of emptiness.

These individuals think in black and white terms. You might be praised one day only to be treated as an enemy the next. This is due to their suspiciousness about the motives of others which they irrationally "confirm" with false assumptions and misinterpretations. You might be treated extremely well when they anticipate a favor, but if it is denied with good reason, you are now the "enemy."

Tactics

Remain calm and detached

Many people have empathy, and feel the emotional pain of others. This reaction will be elicited, but should be resisted with the dramatic because their frequent distress will drain you emotionally. There is not enough empathy in the universe to fill the hole of a dramatic person. Instead, detach yourself emotionally. No matter how much you show them you care, it will never be enough nor will it last. Play the role of the wise grandparent—consoling, but calm and detached. These individuals feel more stable when others around them are grounded. Do not let their highs and lows take you for a ride. Do not take things personally. The dramatic tend to be emotional sponges: any negativity exuded will cause a negative reaction; on the other hand, positive encouragement is likely to be appreciated.

Be assertive to avoid manipulation

The dramatic can appear highly distressed to elicit a desired response. They know that "good people" are generous and empathetic in response to a crisis or someone's distress. It can be hard to tell a tearful person "no" when they appear to be suffering, but it is sometimes necessary. If you are "Johnny-on-the-spot" to do favors, you will be asked for more and more until you are forced to set limits for your own sanity, only to be punished later for "abandoning" them. Instead, set limits from the beginning.

Expect, but do not fall into, the double-bind trap

The "double-bind" is when you are given two options, but whichever one you choose means you lose. It is common for the dramatic to set up lose-lose scenarios for others. Most commonly something like, "I can't make up my mind. You choose." But it is a trap: whatever decision you make will be the "wrong one." Respond by refusing to choose. Reframe it positively by pointing out their competence, e.g. "I have confidence in your ability to choose."

Expose them by pushing their buttons

If you become a target of hostility, others who have not witnessed their dysfunction might be in doubt. If you push their emotional buttons at the right time, in front of others, they are likely to lose control. Those who observe this will begin to view them as having less credibility, while you gain credibility.

Taking Inventory

Ask yourself...

- What makes you vulnerable to selfish or antagonistic people? Is it a desire to be accepted and liked at any price?
- Are you easily intimidated by others? If so, what is the reason?
- Are you willing to give up trying to change others who are unlikely to change?
- Are you willing to use strategy and tactics to manage problem people?
- Can you identify the problem person in your life at this time?
- Is this person one of the antagonistic types?
- Do the rules seem different for them than for you? For example, they can act selfishly, but when you assert your needs you are met with irritability, anger, or indifference?
- Do they act like your hard work or affection is less important to them than some selfish need?

Change Something

Do things differently…

- Make a decision to stop trying to win over the unwinnable.
- Examine your own weaknesses, and if you can, remove them.
- If you cannot remove a weakness or flaw, then boldly accept it, stop hiding it, and stop fearing how others will react!
- Increase your self-confidence to decrease vulnerability.

Develop Wisdom

Think about new strategies…

- Accept that there are people in the world who are successful, but highly selfish.
- Learn the weaknesses of selfish people.
- Look beyond what people say to learn what they are thinking.
- Learn methods to influence others and gain power.

Chapter 3

Law 3: Actions Are Much More Compelling Than Logic

First say to yourself what you would be; and then do what you have to do.

—Epictetus

Most of us realize that rational thinking is an indispensable asset. The successful pursuit of goals requires that we make decisions that are sensible, practical, and feasible. Despite these imperatives, there are many things that people value over rational thinking. What are these things? They all boil down to variations of self-interests rooted in intangibles such as emotions, desires, and prejudices. It is a mistake to underestimate the relevance of these intangibles. Do not expect that others will necessarily appreciate your "objective" and "correct" point of view when it conflicts with their own self-interests. *In order to be successful in social engagement you must accept that self-interest—not rational thought—is the primary basis for human activity.* Sometimes self-interest coincides with rational thought; sometimes it does not.

No one ever admits, "I oppose reasonable plans when they conflict with my self-interests." Instead, they use socially acceptable means to undermine rational ideas, such as arguments that seem credible, but are not. Such arguments can have the effect of creating doubt and confusion in the minds of others. When false arguments cannot work, for example when an idea is obviously correct to everyone, the opposition might use more subtle ways to undermine the idea such as passive-aggressive tactics like procrastination, spreading rumors, or working at a snail's pace to slow down progress. More overt tactics might include attacking the messenger, e.g. "Forget the idea, we cannot trust you," or using distractions, e.g. "That idea is good, but our priority right now is to improve communication among employees." Whenever overt or passive efforts take place to undermine your good ideas, respond by using the best methods to outmaneuver any opposition. The steps to masterfully navigating this aspect of social engagement include: learning the reasons "reason" fails (vulnerability factors); identifying and purging your own misconceptions; appealing to non-rational elements; and acting rather than arguing.

Vulnerability Factors

Those who place a high value on rational thought tend to assume that others will respect their intellect and well-reasoned arguments. This assumption is like a blind spot that makes it harder to notice the many other factors that influence human decision-making. The following are examples of some false and self-defeating assumptions that are common to individuals who over-rely upon rational persuasion...

False assumption # 1: People always appreciate changes for the better

There are many reasons people fear and oppose change, regardless of whether it is ultimately good for themselves or others. Change involves uncertainty, risk, and trust. People fear how change will negatively impact their own interests. Those not included in the implementation of plans are expected to trust others as they patiently and powerlessly wait to see what change means for them.

Less virtuous motivations, such as pride and jealousy, inspire some to fight against new ideas that come from others because they fear that someone else's success will make their light shine brighter than their own. There are those who simply do not want to work harder. A lazy person does not want to find ways to increase efficiency if it means more work. Opposition from a dishonest person arises due to fears of increased accountability. The pride and ego of someone who has put time and effort into creating an existing system could suffer a blow if that system was replaced. These and other fears cause people to resist logical ideas that involve change.

False assumption # 2: Good ideas win, regardless of bad attitudes

Oppositional, antagonistic personalities usually resist sound reasoning when it is not in their self-interest with various expressions of negativity: the pessimists ("It will fail anyhow"), contrarians ("I am right, not you"), passive-aggressive ("I will pretend to agree with you, but resent it and make you pay"), and so forth. When these kinds of personalities hold enough influence they create a social climate of opposition that can sabotage good ideas and actions.

False assumption # 3: The best arguments and explanations ultimately win

Even if you "prove" a point or make a compelling case for something, do not expect others to necessarily agree with you. Some individuals have concealed agendas that they consider much more important than sound reasoning and logical ideas. Such individuals can seldom be won over by explaining—not because they do not understand the basis for a decision, but because something else is more important to them. Signs of this include irrational stubbornness, refusing to dialogue, or an unwillingness to abandon bad ideas. When this happens, stop trying to convince inflexible minds to become flexible. Do not think something like, "If I just explain it for the tenth time he will get it." Pay attention to body language and tone of voice. Try to see the other person's perspective from a self-interested point of view to determine the unspoken reason for their opposition.

False assumption # 4: People will accept hardships for the common good

Expect that what is good for all will be opposed by the few. Sure, sometimes people are willing to make small sacrifices for the common good, but larger sacrifices are usually met with resistance. Do not expect them to be impressed by "big picture" goals when individual self-interests are at stake.

False assumption # 5: Rational ideas speak for themselves

It is sometimes a mistake to think things like, "People will appreciate my good ideas, regardless of whether they like me." Many people judge the message by the messenger. Use your interpersonal skills to help sell your ideas to others and it will reflect well upon you while decreasing negative emotional responses. If you are socially inept or disliked, start by winning over one or two other individuals to your side; later, use them to help advance your ideas and make your case to others.

False assumption # 6: Good reasons carry more weight than emotions

The process of making decisions almost always involves two things: emotion and cognition (thinking). If we only appeal to one of these things, we are less likely to convince others of good ideas. The greatest chance of persuading someone is to combine a logical explanation with an emotional appeal. This is effective because human beings virtually always prefer to act when emotion and reason are congruent. Some version of "It makes sense and you will feel good about it because _____" is much better than a version of "You will like it because it makes sense." Something that is logical, but does not "feel right," is less likely to be accepted.

False assumption # 7: Logical plans and ideas trump politics

Just because an idea is rational does not mean it is politically expedient. If you push a good idea that is politically problematic, you will be perceived as an irritant by self-interested others who will find ways to oppose your efforts and perhaps you personally. Do not just consider how good an idea might be; anticipate all the implications, such as which players will share credit for success or failure; competition for finite resources, and the influence of outside stakeholders. Grease the wheels of your efforts by appeasing those above you in positions of power or authority.

Assess the Challenge

Those who oppose rational ideas are sometimes just being human. Assess someone's true motivation by imagining how a proposed action could impact that individual. Put yourself in their shoes. If it helps, imagine in your mind how others might react if your ideas were successfully implemented. Pay equal attention to how change impacts others and listen to their concerns. This kind of information will help you assess challenges to your success.

You will know if someone is reasonable when there is give and take in a conversation. An acceptable reasonable conversation usually includes explaining an idea, receiving feedback, and making a decision based upon a shared conclusion—or at least "agreeing to disagree" in a civil manner. Unwillingness to engage in rational dialogue, when challenged, is usually met with irritability, interruptions, false counter-arguments, or denial about the facts. These behaviors usually indicate a concealed agenda that is more important to a person than sensible ideas.

Here are some signs to look for when someone is opposing reasonable ideas or plans:

1) They listen and understand, but bring up contrary ideas

without explaining why they are better.

2) They interrupt, act irritable, or make non-specific, dismissive statements, for example, "That's all well and good, but what we should do instead is..."

3) They stubbornly repeat bogus arguments or attempt to intimidate you.

Consider Consequences, Not Just Ideas

Arguments and ideas have been used to justify countless wrongs in this world. Look hard enough and you will find arguments used throughout history, often by highly intelligent and educated individuals, to justify torture, murder, and discrimination. The early twentieth-century communists in Russia, China, and elsewhere murdered millions based on a sophisticated economic philosophy about class inequality and capitalist oppression. In fact, every organized atrocity in modern times has been associated with arguments that were rational in the minds of many. While we might not worry about such atrocities where we live, the point still fits: arguments can be used to justify immoral and irrational actions. Therefore, be alert to sophisticated arguments because they can be used to justify any action. *Guard against false reasoning by scrutinizing possible outcomes.* If an idea seems right, but the effect is ultimately harmful, then the idea might need to be rejected even if it makes sense.

There are certain types who are skilled at using words, but do not have positive intentions. Some appear agreeable, but do not follow through with action. Watch out for those who rely on their appearance or personality rather than substance. They will seduce others with bravado and confidently presented grand ideas, but will shun scrutiny about necessary details. There are also highly intelligent individuals who are prone to theorizing without ever implementing their lofty ideas. The politically savvy will rely on impressing others with promises, but will only follow through if it is to their own benefit. Each of these types of individuals will use some semblance of logic to buttress their arguments, complaints, or promises. Listen, but pay more attention to what their actions would in fact mean if realized. In *every case* ask yourself, "What is the self-interested motive?"

Be careful when someone seems to best you in some discussion or argument. That by itself is not necessarily enough to prove them correct. Pause and imagine what it would be like if that person got his or her way. If the outcome is acceptable to you, with all of its implications, then go with the flow. But if the consequences seem unacceptable, then you should take a stand against it.

Act Instead of Arguing

Actions are more powerful than words. Words are less powerful because they are only sometimes acted upon. For example, every day in the world millions of people grumble about their governments, but few actually make the effort to take action and do anything about it, even something as simple as voting. On the other hand, actions are empirical: when something is demonstrated it cannot be denied. Twenty scientists theorizing about how much a rock weighs would be put to shame by a child who sits it on a scale.

When you discover that you cannot convince someone to do the rational thing through dialogue, explanations, or arguments, you have a free pass to give up on convincing them and move on to other uses of your time and energy. Stop talking; instead, prove to others that you are right with results. Someone else's inaction may leave an opportunity for you to take the initiative and do something. Besides, what is the alternative? When words fail, your choice is to give up or act.

Another benefit of taking action is that it can force someone who opposes you to show their hand. If someone knows that you are close to acting, but they wish to undermine your efforts, your anticipation of this might allow you to catch them in the act. On the other hand, if someone's opposition was a bluff, they are likely to stay out of your way when you actually execute your plans.

Seldom Make Known Your Intentions or Plans

There are times when you need to keep your plans to yourself. When you announce plans or intentions, you open yourself up to criticism because people are likely to point out the pros, cons, risks, and worst-case scenarios of your objectives. The time gap between telling others about your plans and actually implementing them is an opportunity for opposition to begin working against your objectives. Another downside is that if your plan fails, your previous advertising of the plan has drawn unnecessary attention to your failure. If possible, keep a low profile during the planning phase of an activity and play down expectations. If your plan does not succeed, you can always say that you never promised otherwise; however, if your plan succeeds, you can still reap the positive outcome just as much as if you had built up expectations in the first place. Accomplishments are less vulnerable to criticism than plans and ideas. Demonstration after-the-fact is much more compelling than arguments or pitches. Consider the following two sentences and ask yourself which is more powerful:

"I have a plan to accomplish something for our organization."
Or
"I have accomplished something for our organization."

The latter sentence is obviously much more powerful because it described an activity that occurred in reality while the former sentence is merely a plan that may or may not ever occur. The first sentence can be scrutinized and debated; the second, if true, cannot.

Exceptions

There are three exceptions to winning through actions. The first is when a powerful juggernaut—like a government or controlling religious institution—is so invested in false but traditional ideas that any proposed changes will result in persecution (for example, throughout modern history many scientists have been persecuted for disproving established religious and political beliefs).

The second exception occurs when those who resist truth are socially influential. Someone who is famous or known as an "expert" might be biased and able to convince others of their point of view. Usually the truth wins out in the long run, but in the meantime you could suffer social persecution and ridicule from those biased in favor of opinions from "experts," celebrities, and the like.

The third exception is when your actions excel beyond those above you in power or authority in some area where they believe themselves to be superior. Feeling jealous and threatened by your success, they could retaliate. Just as a distinguished professor might not appreciate getting bested by a young student, those above you will not always be grateful for your success. Most of the best books about strategic thinking make this point.

It is especially important to avoid outshining those who have power over you with big egos. Many leaders, experts, professionals, and those who hold some kind of authority over others usually believe that they are superior to others within the little world in which they excel. *Many believe they are not only superior, but that they should be superior to others.* This makes them resent it when others achieve success in areas where they have achieved. A version of this phenomenon happens in some personal relationships. For example, some parents become jealous of their successful or highly intelligent children because they believe the parent should always outshine the child.

Even when someone is equal to you in authority or power it is generally helpful to offset jealous reactions. As an example, imagine a salesman named Nathan who knows how dangerous his success can be. When he sells something he makes sure it is about the product, not his own ego—even though he is an incredibly skilled salesman. When he has the best sales numbers he does not brag about it; instead, he comes up with reasons to share the glory with his supervisor in order to decrease any feelings of envy or resentment. At times he even credits his success to his colleagues by saying things like, "The client was primed by one of you guys," or "I was able to make a sale because one of you told me about a feature the client liked." In the above example Nathan is not only a good salesman but socially prudent. If you act similarly you will mitigate the odds of others targeting you due to fear and envy. Best of all, you can rest assured that deep inside, others will know that you are talented, but they will be glad to work with someone who is humble enough to give others some credit and not brag about it.

Another tactic to mitigate the jealousy of others is to remain humble and point out your minor flaws. An example of this would be a brilliant engineer who—when praised about finishing a job on time—says that he might be a good engineer, but his timing is bad on the golf course, or showing up for meetings on time, or some other minor flaw.

This principle applies in committed relationships. Odds are you do at least one thing much better than your life partner, but if you use this talent to dominate your partner he or she will resent it. Many women, for example, are much more articulate and better arguers than their husbands. The male partner typically responds by shutting down and ends up resenting being overpowered in a contest where the odds are against him. On the other hand, whenever you go to someone else's level and seriously solicit their opinion, they feel listened to and respected, resulting in better diplomacy.

Choose Your Battles

If you frequently complain about this or that injustice, other people will grow weary of your presence, and you will never get the justice you seek. Some will judge you as a petty person or chronic complainer. Injustices happen all of the time and if you look for them, you will find them. Sure, some injustices are intolerable, but generally it is better to focus upon your own responsibilities than to be a crusader for change. If you ignore this wisdom, you will not have allies at your side because people cannot be passionate about every cause. Those above you will be reluctant to promote you out of fear they will become the next object of complaint. If you are always outraged by something, you will perceive yourself as a victim and you will never have inner peace. Accept that the world is unfair and that things like rudeness and favoritism are common. If you cannot be at peace until the world is as you think it should be, then you will never be at peace. A calm mind comes from detaching from things that you cannot control. Seek justice selectively and you will be more successful than if you were fighting for every scrap of it.

Know When to Quit

Some problems are like black holes—they suck your time and energy; even large quantities of resources are never enough. It is always hard to give up working on some project or effort that has been a large investment of your efforts, but the blow to the ego will be easier to tolerate than complete devastation. The statesman Thomas Hobbes once wrote, "It is better to be humbled than ruined." Have the courage and humility to quit when your efforts are going nowhere.

Taking Inventory

Ask yourself…

- Are you prepared to deal with resistance to rational ideas and plans?

- What vulnerabilities do you have as a rational person?

Change Something

Do things differently...

- Stop expecting others to agree with something for the sole reason that it is rational.
- Appeal to self-interest, not merely good ideas.
- Be willing to act, not argue, when words fail.
- Do not necessarily be transparent with your plans.

Develop Wisdom

Consider that...

- Many motivations are more powerful than rational thinking.
- Rational arguments are a double-edged sword: they can be authentic, but they can also have harmful effects when realized.
- People will generally choose self-interests over the good of the many.

Chapter 4

Law 4: Endure a Minor Wrong If It Allows a Much Greater Good

What is morally wrong can never be advantageous, even when it enables you to make some gain that you believe to be to your advantage.
—Marcus Tullius Cicero

Most people think that since they know "right from wrong," they will automatically know the "right thing" to do when necessary. This is a naïve mistake. Having standards is not enough: we must anticipate difficult decisions, conflicts, and uncertainty about the best courses of action. Even when we act according to "morals" or "principles," if our plans are not executed in the right way, we can end up doing more harm than good. Another complication is that we can encounter ruthless or selfish individuals willing to do anything to achieve their goals while the rest of us are limited by standards of conduct. In spite of these concerns, one way to gain confidence about making decisions and solving problems with integrity is to develop new principles that guide the decision-making process. One such principle involves acting according to the *Highest Good*.

Act by Determining the Highest Good

It is a paradoxical fact that standards of conduct sometimes seem to contradict themselves. Dilemmas of this sort are fairly common: whether to be honest if it could hurt someone emotionally; whether to cover up misbehavior out of loyalty to a friend; whether to help one person when it means we cannot help someone else, etc. In such circumstances it is best to base your decision on the *Highest Good* defined as: the maximum amount of good that can be accomplished. Making a decision according to the Highest Good involves four steps: a) assessing all possible actions, b) hypothesizing possible outcomes for each action, c) identifying which of several possible actions would produce maximal good, and d) using any means necessary to implement that action. The Highest Good helps us choose between different complicated scenarios, some of which are described as follows.

Use the Highest Good to justify questionable methods

Many paragons of morality in modern history used questionable methods to achieve great things. Consider how Gandhi, Martin Luther King, Vaclav Havel, and many others used civil disobedience tactics, including violating laws, in their efforts to protest certain injustices. Such individuals did not enjoy breaking laws; rather, they had decided that as a last resort the pursuit of freedom, rights, and justice is even a higher good than obeying the law. Some laws they viewed as unjust and therefore invalid. Just like them, the rest of us sometimes face situations that require breaking some kind of rule in order to obtain a much higher good. The following scenario illustrates this point.

Jon works at a bank. The bank manager has "issues," personally dislikes Jon, and has been looking for excuses to fire him for no good reason. Somehow Jon made a mistake and at the end of his shift his count was under by $100. He's not sure, but he thinks he accidentally gave a customer an extra $100 bill. New money sometimes sticks together. He rarely makes mistakes. By policy, he needs to report it, but if he does, he will probably get fired. His choices include being honest—and possibly getting fired—or concealing his mistake. Jon takes $100 out of his own wallet, slips it into his till, and submits it as balanced.

Before we judge Jon as being "deceptive," imagine that he is a good man fallen on hard times. He is the sole provider for his family, two months behind on his mortgage, and would likely have a difficult time finding another job. Being honest is small consolation if it means you are unemployed and your family is homeless. Jon made his decision to put $100 into the till based on his assessment of the Highest Good: he considered the welfare of his family much more important than admitting an unintentional, rare mistake. He even used his own money to cover up the mistake.

It might be argued that Jon risked getting into trouble anyhow if the customer he mistakenly gave the extra $100 to was honest enough to come back to the bank to report the error and give the money back. But even if that happened, Jon could lie and deny it by insisting his count was correct. Doing so would make it much harder for his supervisor to fire him because there would be no proof that Jon made the error over the customer. Furthermore, as a general rule if you expect people to be honest when it comes to free money, you will more often be wrong than right. Jon would not have been wise to assume that the average customer would be so honest as to return the money.

Jon had a dilemma that in general is fairly common: whether to use deception for some higher purpose and greater good. Someone other than Jon might have decided, out of principle, to be honest no matter the consequences. It is up to us as individuals to decide what the Highest Good is in every situation. This awareness allows us to act with greater confidence and a clear conscience.

In determining the Highest Good it is necessary to anticipate consequences and effects. To illustrate this point, recall that during World War II many European families hid Jews in their homes to protect them from the Nazis. The Nazis knew about this effort and sometimes went from house to house, looking for Jews and collaborators. For most, it would have been immoral to decide, "It is always wrong to lie; therefore, if the Nazis ask whether Jews are hidden in my house, I must admit it." To do so would have resulted in the deaths or imprisonment of the Jews and possibly those hiding them. In that situation preserving human life was considered a higher good than telling the truth. Those who considered this dilemma ahead of time were prepared to make their decision.

While the above example is definitely a type of worst-case scenario, there are other instances where deception is used to attain the Highest Good. Ask yourself whether you have any problems with the following actions:

- A boxer faking out his opponent
- Someone putting on their best airs during a job interview or first date
- Telling a lie to protect someone from harm
- An undercover spy lying about his identity
- Telling a distressed child "Things will be all right" when that is not certain
- A business advertising "the best deals" without bothering to find out if that is a fact
- On a rare occasion, calling in sick when you are not, just to keep one's sanity

Consider that while nearly everyone has used some form of benign deception, most people operate on "autopilot" and do not think about the wider scope of their actions, resulting in confusion and uncertainty whenever two competing ideas are at odds with each other. Instead of avoiding the subject, develop your own template of the Highest Good and follow it consistently. Avoid simple conformity and remember that no one has the right to tell you what your Highest Good should be. Do not use the Highest Good as an excuse to get away with lying; if you do, you will descend a slippery slope toward losing your ethical bearing and end up telling one lie to cover another, which will eventually catch up with you. It is only with reluctance that anyone should endure minor deviations from honesty.

Use of the Highest Good can also help us make complicated decisions. Sometimes we need to choose between the common and individual good, or between two positive or negative outcomes. There are also situations where short-term good conflicts with long-term good. For example, should employees be given a bonus or should it go to paying down debt? Should I let my wife continue to depend upon me for making the important decisions, or encourage her independence and give up control? In each case, determining the Highest Good will allow you to make the decision that is most likely to maximize a desired outcome. This can be done with integrity, even if the methods used mean that we must endure a minor wrong to accomplish something.

Strategy and Power Are Amoral

Unfortunately, success does not necessarily depend upon morality. As proof, consider that history is filled with accounts of kings, generals, politicians, and business leaders who attained and kept power with utter ruthlessness—without morality. Many used deception, fear, or criminal acts to accomplish their goals. The opposite is also true: the morality of many great leaders contributed to their success. Virtue earns trust, respect, and devotion; sometimes even love. However, most, if not all noteworthy historical figures used a blending of styles. The most violent, Machiavellian leaders still had to be self-disciplined and skilled enough to accomplish their aims. Not just anyone could be killed or threatened. On the other hand, many virtuous leaders had to make exceptions to justice for a higher purpose. Compromises, back-door deals, legal maneuvers, and bribery are all methods that have been used by virtuous leaders to achieve noble aims—often because there was no alternative. Even the best of us seldom let the perfect become the enemy of the good.

Strategy and power are neither moral nor immoral; that is to say, they are amoral. *Strategy and power can be compared to a game of chess: even if the devil and an angel played against each other, the only things that would matter are the rules of the game and the skill of the players.* In our world, the "rules" are the facts we cannot change; that is, things we have no control over. "Skill" includes the strategy and tactics that we use to increase our chances of success. Whether moral or ruthless, success is more likely with good planning and methods. Thus it is very important for those with integrity to learn how to think strategically. Of course there are times when we must choose to do the right thing in spite of loss, but with the help of proper strategic thinking these instances of loss should be reduced to a tiny number.

Power, like strategy, is amoral. If we continue with the above analogy, power in the game of chess consists of how much of the board is controlled by one player and the ability to move pieces. Similarly, exercising power is the ability to accomplish a specific objective. Power underlies all human activity—from the largest organizations down to individuals working together in obscure groups. The use of power is a matter of preference: it can be used for good or harm. In any case, nearly all forms of success depend upon the acquisition and proper use of power. If you cannot control or influence others, you must either work alone or rely on luck or charity for your success. Reliance on luck and charity alone are poor strategies indeed! That few understand the nature of power explains the fact that, regardless of all the effort that many put into life, the majority of us have difficulty protecting what we possess, and even fewer of us increase what we have.

Many eminent thinkers have argued that the successful exercising of power requires a separation of morals from strategy. Henry Kissinger, for example, perhaps the greatest American diplomat of the twentieth century, believed that morality is irrelevant in politics and foreign policy. The Italian Renaissance diplomat and father of modern political science, Niccolò Machiavelli, argued that an aspiring prince should be ruthless and cunning in order to attain and preserve power and influence.

While it is true that these men and other important thinkers have claimed that immoral methods are sometimes needed in order to achieve a desirable outcome, their ideas are frequently misunderstood. Few have ever argued that it is possible for someone with authentic integrity to completely suppress their values and beliefs. On a personal level, Kissinger and Machiavelli were hardly amoral; in fact, they desired peace and hoped for a better future world. Kissinger believed in Western values like democracy and desired to see the defeat of oppressive regimes; Machiavelli wanted peace and unity achieved between powerful, feuding Italian families. The lengths that these men and others would go to achieve their goals is always a question of moral scrutiny.

Another important point made by thinkers like Machiavelli and Kissinger is that *moral uncertainty can sabotage a larger moral victory*. When people are unclear about what they are willing and unwilling to do, they inevitably find themselves temporarily confused, indecisive, and unable to act quickly enough to be successful. Of course no one has a right on a personal level to lecture you about your own standards of conduct, but you do have an obligation to yourself to get specific about your principles. If you nail down how far you are willing to go in your efforts to achieve your goals, you will be better able to handle novel situations as they arise.

Purge Moral Hang-Ups

Moral uncertainty sometimes results from our own moral hang-ups. Principles and standards are only guides that point us in the right direction; beyond that, there is nothing that can tell us with specific precision the exact, correct decision to make every time. Even teachers of strict religions quibble among themselves about topics not explicitly addressed in their religious writings and traditions. But for many of us a lack of clarity can sometimes cause our sense of morality to become convoluted by self-defeating hang-ups and irrational ideas. Do not get caught up in minutiae or second-guess yourself all the time. Like Alexander the Great who cut the Gordian knot, get to the heart of the matter, see the big picture, and act according to the Highest Good. If you over-think your decisions you will be slow, inefficient, and doubt yourself, resulting in low self-confidence.

Moral hang-up # 1: You should not be worldly or ambitious

Having morals does not mean that someone should not value pleasure, power, status, money, or any of the multitudes of worldly blessings that one can possess—it just means that these things are not considered among the *very most* important things in life. Get rid of this hang-up by noticing how your values help prioritize your life. Things like personal integrity, family, friends, and meaningful work might be the most important things to you, but there is nothing wrong with a drive to get promoted, make more money, or have the pleasures you desire. Worldly ambitions are compatible with morality. We can prioritize the most important things in life without necessarily excluding other desires. In fact, much good can be accomplished when we direct whatever worldly ambitions we have for a higher purpose.

Moral hang-up # 2: You should strive for moral perfection

Striving for moral perfection is a well-intentioned mistake. In reality, the complexities of life make achieving moral perfection impossible. This is a fact because moral principles sometimes conflict with each other. For example, there are circumstances where telling the truth could harm someone, but telling a lie protects them. Moreover, no one is perfect. Those who excessively scrutinize their own intentions and actions tend to be indecisive and ineffective.

It is especially important to find a way to be morally flexible when engaging antagonistic or hostile people. In order to illustrate this point, imagine that you are lost in the middle of the ocean, alone, and your boat starts to capsize. Your only choices include drowning or swimming to a nearby island. You happen to know that the only inhabitants on this island are psychopaths exiled by a mainland government 1000 miles away. No one who lives there has any morality. Treachery, greed, and selfishness are the norm. Only the strong survive. You finally make your way to the island and come to your senses. You will not be able to leave until the next ferry arrives in six months. You know that in the months to come if you insist upon acting morally perfect, you will not survive. Yet you cannot become like them: you must find a way to survive without sacrificing your integrity.

Just like the person in this story, there are times in the real world when we find ourselves outnumbered or trapped in situations with selfish and antagonistic individuals. It might be a new job or a dysfunctional family reunion. In such circumstances it is unwise to consistently display morally perfect traits like generosity or giving others the benefit of the doubt. Instead, survival—at least on a psychological level—requires us to be cautious and skeptical about the motivations of others.

Moral hang-up # 3: Honesty requires transparent disclosure

Honesty does not mean that one needs to be "an open book" for the world to see. It is necessary to conceal many things from others—not to be deceptive but for healthy boundaries. Some people believe that if you have nothing to hide you should disclose any information asked of you or live an "exposed" life, open to the scrutiny of others. This is a mistake for several reasons. For instance, you are likely to be less respected because many people believe that privacy should be valued and that if you are an honest person you do not need to prove it to anybody.

Also, people who are honest to a fault end up calling unnecessary attention to their mistakes. When they do, others will notice their errors, but not respect them for their honesty.

Real-life example of excessive honesty

"Greg" had recently started taking a new medication and did not know that it increased the effects of alcohol. While using his computer at home, he poured himself a glass of wine. After his second glass he got a little delirious, began surfing the internet, and anonymously flirted with his supervisor's spouse on social media. The next morning, he felt guilty and went to his supervisor and confessed his indiscretion. He stated, "I have to confess, I made a huge mistake the other night and found myself flirting with your wife. I think it was due to my new medication. Please forgive me." His supervisor responded by saying, "Hmm. Thanks for telling me. Let me get back to you." At the end of Greg's nervous shift he was greeted by company security who informed him he had been terminated; they then escorted him to his car on the orders of Greg's supervisor.

Do not end up like Greg by confessing to a fault no one would discover otherwise, unless you can think of some real good it would do for yourself or others.

Moral hang-up # 4: It is always right to ease the suffering of others

Just like a physician's injection causes pain, but to heal or inoculate, there are times when doing the right thing causes pain for someone you know. Examples of this include ending unhealthy relationships, putting limits on generosity, and ending enabling behaviors that have made someone overly dependent. Think about this analogy: when a toddler screams every time he or she does not get candy, only a stupid parent would say, "Poor thing. I do not want to see you suffer so I will get you candy every time you want it." That statement is obviously wrong and would be a form of enabling that in the long term would make a child sick, overweight, and diabetic. But enabling is actually very common in adult relationships. People stay in relationships where they have been miserable for years because they worry about the other person's reaction to leaving them. Get unstuck from this kind of situation by realizing that just because someone resists, complains, or becomes distressed does not mean that they should get their way. This is a form of manipulation. Be willing to make hard decisions, even when the result is the short-term unhappiness of someone else; in return, you will get long-term sanity.

Accept Minor Moral Imperfections

Another complexity involves the minutiae of simply being human. Which one of us has never called in sick to work when we were feeling just fine? Which one of us has never told a white lie to avoid trouble, hide mistakes, save time, or make someone feel better? Which one of us has never been a little lazy, undisciplined, or short-tempered? Throw in some instances of complaining, gossiping, and putting off our responsibilities... face it, each of us is far from perfect. Be honest, admit your shortcomings, and you will be a better person for it. Doing so allows you to get unstuck from self-scrutiny and self-pity.

Avoid the Extremes of Excessive Ambition and Passivity

"Success" is like beauty: it takes countless forms and is different to all. For some, it simply means survival, security, and safety from predation. A minority are not content to live in peace and wish to exercise their ambition to attain something above their current circumstances. Some vacillate between these emphases; ambitious when younger, but preferring contentment when mature. Thus, human aspirations can be classified in three ways:

self-protecting, aggrandizing, or a combination of both. The following describes the preferences of some individuals followed by a recommendation for flexibility.

Lovers of peace

Many people desire to live peaceful lives and focus upon protecting what they have already attained. Preferring to avoid problems, they seek security; only when necessary do they engage conflict. Such people value social harmony and a calm mind over status or material things. They dislike ambitious struggles and stressful conflict. They are not lazy, but will stop exerting themselves once a certain set of goals have been achieved. This type of person, when successful, is a bringer of stability—not like those who act like much is never enough.

The ambitious

The second kind of individual desires a higher station in life beyond a moderate degree of comfort and security. Such individuals are seldom content as there is always another goal to achieve, but their efforts can produce the greatest results. They will not shirk from conflict and can thrive in highly competitive environments. As a force for good, their confidence and ability to take risks can lead to wonderful achievements. On the other hand, this type of person is inevitably tempted to go beyond what is good, resulting in unnecessary hardships for themselves and others.

Use a combined approach

Life is unpredictable; therefore, flexibility is needed. A combined approach of the above two types is more likely to ensure success. It is best to avoid extremes: human beings need challenges, but too much ambition means that someone is prizing personal accomplishments over the good of others. Not being ambitious at all is bad too—it leads to stagnation and laziness. A wise and principled person avoids extremes and knows when to proceed and when to refrain, regardless of personal preference. Recognize which of the above styles is yours by nature, but accept that your success may depend upon your ability to be flexible. "There is a time for peace and a time for war."

Thus far we have outlined the most general objectives of human aspirations:

1) To protect what one has
2) To acquire more of what one values

We have observed that individuals may prefer 1 or 2, but success depends upon not overemphasizing one approach over another in an extreme way.

Conclusion

If you want to make a positive difference in this world, you must be willing to endure minor wrongs to achieve higher goods. Know how to do this by developing and prioritizing your template of the Highest Good. There are times when you will have to weigh whether the end goal justifies the means to achieve it. But that is an individual choice based on your values and no one has the right to decide things for you. The important thing to do is to think about your actions in the big picture. Make a decision about your values and the methods you are willing to use to succeed. The vast majority of people live life on "autopilot," never stopping to think about these kinds of things, and end up struggling when confronted with novel, complex, and difficult situations.

Taking Inventory

Ask yourself…

- Do you know what to do when acting upon your principles

might result in undesirable outcomes?
- Do you have moral hang-ups?
- Are you honest or generous to a fault?

Change Something

Do things differently...

- Tailored to your own principles, use the doctrine of the Highest Good to make complicated decisions.
- Purge yourself of moral hang-ups and embrace clear principles.
- Accept moral imperfections rather than getting hung up on them.
- Be flexible, regardless of your preference for an ambitious or tranquil life.

Develop Wisdom

Consider that...

- Power and strategy are amoral (neither moral nor immoral).
- It is how we use power and strategy for good or bad that really counts.
- Goal achievement requires mental flexibility and adaptable principles.

Chapter 5

Law 5: The Majority Are Impressed with the Superficial

The appearance is seldom the reality.
—Plato

In order to know the true meanings of things we must look beyond mere appearances. Even our primitive ancestors must have understood this when they noticed that a straight stick held underwater looks bent when it is not. In our time, there are many social "sticks," that is, discrepancies between any person you see and the real person. Each of us wears a "mask" that hides our true selves. Those who are manipulative and selfish hide their true motivations beneath this "mask" and attempt to convince others that they actually have excellent characters and good intentions. The power of surface appraisals makes us vulnerable to deception; therefore, successful strategic engagement requires that we avoid deception by looking beyond mere impressions.

Look closely and you will notice that on a daily basis people are highly influenced by superficial impressions. Advertising, for example, seldom tells us anything meaningful about products, yet it is a multibillion-dollar industry with proven effectiveness. Television, radio, and even the people we know give out uninformed opinions as if they were facts. All forms of media create impressions upon the mind. Those who proudly argue that they are not influenced by such things can easily recall a song from an advertisement or identify a corporate logo. This is because a repeated exposure to something creates an impression in our minds, influencing us to act in a desired manner.

One of the reasons that impressions are so powerful is how we evolved as a species. Our ancestors did not have the luxury to hesitate when hungry or afraid; resources were scarce and danger was ever-present. Thus we are hard-wired to make snap evaluations about whatever we perceive with our senses. The twig swaying in the breeze could be a lion's tail. Most of us may not have such concerns in the modern world, but we are still required to make snap judgments. Technology has made life fast-paced with sources of stimulation all around us. Who has time to dig beneath the surface? Imagine the labors of someone attempting to track down the "truth" about every piece of news they read or heard in even a single day.

You Are a Mini-Brand

The pervasiveness of social media has made billions of individual profiles accessible to others. If you are on social media, use it to your advantage; if not, you are missing a huge opportunity to influence how others perceive you. People in general expect you to be on social media; those who ignore this vital fact will be increasingly ignored and marginalized. Do not be like the dying paper phone-book in a world where people "google" everything they want to know about on computers and smartphones. You should consider yourself a "mini-brand" that requires proper marketing. Assume that your name is what people search for on the internet after they first meet you, learn about your work, and after you have applied for a job. Your online image might not help people know the "real you," but it does provide a first, critical impression that will open or close doors of opportunity.

> Men judge generally more by the eye than by the hand, because it belongs to everybody to see you, few to come in touch with you. Everyone sees what you appear to be; few really know what you are.
> —Niccolò Machiavelli

Convey the Right Image

Like it or not, a person's mannerisms, appearance, style of writing or speaking, or how they present in person or on social media formats can at first carry more weight than positive qualities like self-discipline, critical thinking skills, and a good work ethic. How you immediately appear is known quickly; your true character is only known with time. It is therefore necessary to find a way to remain authentic in a world where surface impressions get noticed. One mistake some people make is to assume that an "authentic" person should not "sell out" by manipulating superficialities. This is a mistake because no one can see your naked soul or hope to know the "real you" unless they get to know you personally over time. Do not shun the superficial as unseemly or beneath your dignity. Most people form opinions based upon what they immediately see before digging deeper—if they ever do. Thus it is important to take control of how you want to be perceived.

"You" would still be "you" even if you changed your clothing, habits, or the exact way you speak or express your feelings. It is possible to be an authentic person regardless of whether you change these things entirely. Swallow your pride, look in the mirror, and ask yourself if there is anything you can do to improve the impression you convey to others. An inferior image only detracts from a higher purpose. Do not let your personal hang-ups or proclivities get in the way of your success. *Appear as you want to be perceived.* If you want to be a certain kind of person, close your eyes and imagine how you think most individuals would conceive of what that person acts and looks like, then attempt to conform to that image. An aspiring lawyer should not look like a stoner at a rock concert. Do not go overboard and forget who you are and where you come from, but recognize the role you need to play and do it well.

Remove Minor Imperfections

It is a common mistake to believe that others will *only* perceive you in a better light after you have accomplished something. People are easily swayed by appearances and this should be used to your advantage. Eliminate the little indiscretions that call attention to themselves. Work on abandoning bad habits and begin acting in the manner that you want to be perceived. Someone who giggles all the time will not be taken seriously; someone who apologizes too much will appear to have low self-confidence; someone who dresses like a slob will not appear professional; someone who talks too much is annoying. We all have or have had some minor flaw that by itself seems innocent, but is just one more thing that detracts from a higher purpose, namely, your personal goals. Purge yourself of minor imperfections that get in the way of the impression that you wish to convey.

There are those who believe that "being real" means acting however they feel and expressing their opinions regardless of how it ends up offending others. Such individuals take pride in their brutal honesty, which is really just a form of bowing out of the social game where subtleties count. In the process, people consider them prone to offending others and exclude them from opportunities, but never tell them about it in order to avoid conflict. Those who think that outward conformity means someone is inauthentic are mistaken because our opinions, values, and unique perspectives begin in the mind, not outside the mind.

When others criticize you, swallow your pride and seriously consider whether you need self-improvement. When a well-meaning person takes you aside and suggests that you change something about how you present to others, accept this advice as golden. It is hard to accurately judge how we are perceived by others; therefore, feedback can be precious. Ask for feedback at the right time from the right person and take it seriously.

Do Not Be Seduced by Appearances

Manipulating superficialities is a way of placating the weaknesses of others. Use them to your advantage, but do not take them seriously or be moved by affectation. If you are easily impressed by the mere appearances of things you will lose focus upon your ultimate goal. Many individuals with potential have been thrown off course by being seduced by the fake and obvious rather than the hidden and real. This is especially true of someone beginning to make progress in the acquisition of power. Money, popularity, status, pleasure—or in fact any desirable thing—should be considered resources or perks on the path to acquiring your version of success. If you become seduced by them you risk losing everything—at best you will end up settling for less.

But while the majority of people are impressed by appearances, the wise are not. The ancient Roman philosopher Epictetus said that no one should be impressed by a man who owns a fine horse (modern equivalent = expensive car) because it indicates nothing at all about the owner. He observed that while it makes sense to appreciate the horse, nothing more can be concluded. You should take the same attitude toward others. Do not be impressed simply because someone has this or that blessing in life. Most people become intimidated by the success of others, but the opposite reaction is actually more rational: you should be suspicious about whether their prosperity was deserved. If only individuals of merit and good character were successful, the world would be a much better place than it is today. Society is complex and every variable is mixed. Family wealth has made millionaires of idiots while in other parts of the world geniuses go hungry. In some parts of the world saints get murdered while murderers rule. We like to believe that successful individuals are also virtuous, but history shows that there is no correlation between worldly success and scruples. There have been many powerful men and women who did not hesitate to kill their own sons or daughters or starve their own people to maintain power.

But there have always been impoverished families who gladly shared with another person what little they had. Thus, you should never be intimidated by the prestige or success of others. Of course you should *act* in a manner that reflects your social role, but without internally being impressed by externals. It would be reasonable, for example, to treat a senator with high respect, even if he or she was a scoundrel.

When speaking to men of consequence it is necessary to look on them with contempt and not to be impressed by their lofty position.
—Mencius

Those who choose not to follow this advice find that everything that impresses them undermines their focus. If you value money too much how can you remain calm and determined when exposed to wealth? If you are preoccupied with status how can you interact naturally with someone of high position? If you are preoccupied with sexual attraction how can you calmly appeal to the person of your affection? Of course each of us can choose to pursue our desires, but success requires focused effort. During combat it would be dangerous for a soldier to think about victory spoils more than survival. Mentally detach from those desires which might distract you in the moment. Let others be influenced by externals, but you must not take them too seriously. Appearances are always a means to an end. The very wisest individuals despise everything that is not related to their ultimate objective.

Be Skeptical of Superficial Charm

There is no greater joy for me to find, on self-examination, that I am true to myself.
—Mencius

Charm is a successful method used by manipulators. They can seem alluring, pleasing, witty, fun-loving, confident, and even charismatic. At first, they will assess your needs, wants, and weaknesses. Like a chameleon, they will then use this information to assume a pleasing form. If someone is a talker, they will be a good listener; if someone is lonely, they will act like a friend; if someone needs emotional support, they will provide it. But for manipulators these are only tactics used in passing to obtain some kind of selfish interest. The person who has been seduced is merely an object to be discarded when no longer of use.

To protect yourself from manipulation, do the opposite of others: *the greater the charm, the more suspicious you should be*. But do not let others know that you are suspicious; after all, you could be wrong. Be outwardly accepting of charm, but internally skeptical. When possible, "test" the intentions of another person. For example, if possible, let them think that you might not be of any use to them and see whether or not they remain interested in you. Another option is to lure them with their object of desire while at the same time acting irritable or argumentative toward them; a "normal" person would be bothered, but those who remain sweet and charming could be manipulative.

What people say and do is sometimes a smokescreen for something else. If you only accept the obvious, you will not really understand underlying social dynamics. Someone with a hidden agenda will always appear to have good reasons for doing something, but the true motive could be entirely selfish. Dig a little deeper and you will understand the realities of social nuances. So how can you tell what is hidden? There are two primary ways to become a more discerning person; these include: *discerning the hidden message* and *decoding the rules*.

Look Beyond Words to Discern Hidden Messages

What someone says is only like a transcript, the mere content of words, and not to be trusted at face value. Most words spoken by people are only superficial descriptions or opinions and do not communicate the underlying social and political realities of human interaction. The concealed, unspoken message is the real message. This is sometimes called "meta-communication."

Consider the following scenario:

Kristy was a hard-working, paid staffer for a member of Congress. After the congressman won election, Kristy remembered how many times he said he appreciated her hard work and would always remember her. Over the course of a month she sent him two emails and left one voicemail asking for help getting a good reference for a new job. He never replied to her communication, but fortunately she was able to meet him at a local event. He greeted her with a smile, but frowned when she asked about help getting a job. He said that he did not know if he could help her, that he was very busy, but that he might call her within about a month. He quickly moved on to talking to other people. He never called.

In the above scenario, if on the day of their encounter Kristy only paid attention to the politician's words she could logically conclude something like, "He's a busy man, but I know that he's still willing to help me because he would call me." But the real message the politician was sending her was, "I have no interest in you or helping you." A downcast facial expression and delayed or ignored replies usually indicate that someone is not interested in helping you.

If you are unsure about whether someone is using meta-communication, here are some questions to consider: Is there a difference between a person's verbal and non-verbal behavior? What is the real motive behind someone's words or actions? Based on what you know about this person, is there a discrepancy between how they are behaving now and how you would expect them to act?

Decode the Rules

Another subtle aspect of social engagement involves understanding the difference between explicit and unwritten rules.
Explicit rules include standards of conduct that are openly
communicated, for example, the policies of an organization,
ethical standards, laws, and written agreements. Unwritten rules
are expectations people have that are supposed to be known,
even if they are not spoken out loud. Due to hypocrisy and
double standards, often there is a huge discrepancy between
explicit and unwritten rules. For example, the policy, "Employees
will be promoted based on merit" sounds impressive, but
management might operate according to the unspoken rule,
"Regardless of merit, management promotes people they
personally like and spend time with outside of work." Another
common example is the following confusing discrepancy:
"Employees are entitled to three weeks of vacation a year,"
versus "Taking more than one week off at a time is frowned
upon." Of course seldom do people openly admit these kinds of
discrepancies, even when everyone knows they are true—they
are *unwritten rules*.

Do not be naïve. *Most social interactions involve unspoken rules
that virtually no one discusses openly.* Those who do not pick up on
unwritten rules are likely to experience subtle forms of persecution from others. They are usually perceived as either clueless
or troublemakers. Make it a priority to figure out the unwritten
rules in every social situation. Just like words, actions too need to
be decoded. An easy example to think about is "Don't invade my
personal space." More difficult ones include unwritten rules held
by individuals, for example, "I will treat you bad as long as we
are competing for the same position."

Whenever you figure out an unwritten rule, it helps if you can
put it into a sentence. Most of the time this will come easily, but
sometimes it is necessary to ponder what the real versus hidden
message might be over time. This includes within the context of

personal relationships. Consider the following scenario:

> *For the last three years Sally has wanted Tom to propose to her.*
> *During that time, she has been out of work and living off of Tom's*
> *income. She has excessively shopped and spent Tom's money,*
> *despite their financial struggles. Whenever he tells her to stop*
> *spending so much money she gets irritable and complains about his*
> *lack of commitment.*

The unwritten rule in the above situation from Sally's point of view might be, "I am justified in spending a lot of Tom's money because I resent that he will not marry me." Another version might be, "His lack of commitment causes me pain, so I will cause him pain by spending his money." If Tom is like most individuals, he would never agree to such a rule if it were explicit. If Tom never decodes the rule and just reacts angrily on a situational basis, he will not see the connection between Sally's behavior and his reluctance to marry her. Similarly, if Sally is not a self-aware person she might "know" she is resentful about Tom's lack of commitment, but she might not connect her feelings of resentment to her excessive spending.

Decoding rules gives you power. It allows you to see clearly what is going on by putting social dynamics into one simple sentence. This knowledge allows you to know what is really going on, forcing others to either deny or admit the truth. This is like "calling a spade a spade." Conflict can only be resolved when people get to the heart of matters instead of dancing around them.

Sympathy Can Be a Superficial Sentiment

It is for some shocking to learn that even tender human feelings can be overshadowed by social pressures or other stressors. Under the right circumstances, sincere qualities like kindness, generosity, loyalty, sympathy, and even love can be less influential than selfishness or hostility.

> In the early days of the Holocaust, Nazi prison guards sometimes wept as they mowed down Jewish women and children, but they still did it. Subjects in the famous Milgram experiments felt anguish as they appeared to administer electric shocks to other research subjects, but they pressed on because some guy in a lab coat told them to.
> *New York Times* article, 2011

Sympathy means having compassion or feeling sorry about someone else's suffering. It is an essential ingredient for human morality, but like flour in a cake, by itself, one ingredient is not enough. It can be trumped by selfish sentiments. As hard as it might be to believe, the truth is that someone might care about you, feel your pain, and even possess a sense of right and wrong—*and none of these things will necessarily stop them from acting selfishly*. As noted in Chapter 1, this is possible because human beings by nature struggle with conformity and are prone to act selfishly when fearful, or under stress, or when we feel threatened by competition. Occasionally the problem is not overt selfishness, but inaction. In highly dysfunctional environments even the most responsible person might become overwhelmed by problems and stop acting in a helpful manner—just like an exasperated mother of six children who has stopped running whenever a child starts crying. As you ring the alarm bell about your suffering, nothing happens because the other person has been desensitized or overwhelmed by other burdens. The bottom line is that you should pay attention to someone's actions more than anything else. Just because someone shares your values and sympathizes with your suffering does not mean that they will intervene to help you.

Forgiveness Can Be a Superficial Sentiment

Do not assume that someone has forgiven you. Even if you have forgiven someone, do not assume reciprocity. True forgiveness is hard to do and rare in this world. Most people who sincerely forgive still end up holding onto little pieces of resentment. The intent to "forgive and forget" does not destroy the neurons in our brain that hold the memories of past betrayals and psychological injuries. "Forgive and forget" is more accurately "forgive and try to let go of painful memories." When someone says they have forgiven you, it is easy for those memories to resurface and trigger resentments.

Self-Interest is a better predictor of future behavior than hearing "I forgive you"

We cannot see into the heart of a person to know whether real forgiveness has occurred, but we can know how someone benefits from keeping a relationship. People will usually tolerate many negative things if they think it is to their advantage. If someone has a hard time forgiving another person, but nonetheless finds keeping the relationship advantageous, then it is possible to get along with that person as they are willing to set aside their resentment. Self-interest is so powerful it can supplant and heal emotional wounds. It is even possible for two people who hate each other to work together to solve a common problem. But be careful—resentments reemerge as soon as the shared self-interested motive goes away.

None Are Immune

It is mistaken to believe that if you work for a non-profit, hospital, or in a helping profession that you are protected from selfish colleagues. Certainly those around you might outwardly espouse enlightened values, but that does not mean they are saints. In fact, some of the worst documented cases of adults bullying and intimidating their co-workers come from the nursing and religious professions. Hospitals call it "horizontal violence" and due to the stress it creates it is associated with medication errors and poor decision-making. This phenomenon is only beginning to be studied by organizations like the Joint Commission (the accrediting organization for hospitals in the United States). Similarly, it is common for pastors to complain about burnout and a desire to leave their vocation due to selfishness and infighting in their many congregations.

Wisdom Is Higher Than Superficial Traits

Qualities such as competency, agreeableness, and good judgment make us useful and appreciated by others. On a deep level, rarely acknowledged, most people respect these traits over someone who makes them laugh, buys drinks, drives a fast car, or knows how to keep a conversation going. Think of it this way: when there is a crisis, do people look for someone who is only known as the "pretty lady," or the "funny co-worker," or the "story-teller"? No. Instead, they look for someone who is a problem-solver, or has good judgment, or can remain calm while making decisions. When someone needs advice, they look for the good listener, the empathic, or the experienced. When someone is scared they seek the company of those who tell the truth and do not want to harm them. There are many virtues: prudence, patience, creativity, perseverance, etc. Make an active effort to cultivate your key virtues and let them shine before others. Remember that for every situation there is a particular virtue that can be of help. Whenever there is a crisis or you have to make a big decision, ask yourself what virtue is called for in that situation. This will help you know what to do. Remember that lesser qualities are not as valued, even if they get more attention. If you develop many virtues in addition to possessing good judgment, then you will eventually transcend to a position of wisdom. You may or may not get invited to more parties, but others will learn to respect you, which is ultimately more valuable than being entertaining. And even if you are not more respected, deep down inside you know, and others know, that you have something of worth that they most likely do not possess to the same degree.

Wisdom Is Higher Than Knowledge

Knowledge and intellect are indispensable, but they are not necessarily enough to help someone be successful in social engagement. Sometimes intellectuals live "in their heads," theorize without acting, and remain socially awkward. Some people read many books about self-improvement without making any progress in life. There are those who are smart and capable, but lack emotional maturity. Even a child who is a genius has much to learn in life. Moreover, knowledge and intellect are irrelevant to someone's intentions. Some of the most brilliant individuals in history have been the most destructive. Wisdom, however, requires an understanding of the "big picture" in life. No one is considered wise who is selfish. Some of the wisest men and women in human history had little technology and some could not even read or write, but they understood what was right and wrong and beneficial or harmful for themselves and those around them.

Wisdom helps us solve problems by helping us understand what is at the heart of the matter and beyond impressions. Do not lose focus with distractions, which results in frustration. Set aside the trivial when important tasks are at hand. The hunter, when aiming his weapon, does not worry about mosquitoes. Learn the art of succinct speech: if you can say in one or two sentences what takes others a long, rambling digression, then you are on your way to mastering how to grasp what is the essence of something.

Wisdom Is Higher Than Wit

Better to be wise than witty. The jokester might receive positive attention from others on a daily basis, but jocularity does not cultivate true respect. No one looks to the witty person about matters of importance or during a crisis. Thus the saying is true, "Wisdom is higher than wit." Remember, even if others do not seem to appreciate skill or wisdom over wit, deep down inside people know who possesses good judgment. The clown gets more laughs, and therefore more attention, but the skilled person is more respected, even if it is never spoken or acknowledged.

Do Not Be Defined by Superficial Terms

People tend to take shortcuts in language when describing another person: "He is the loud one," "She is the talker," "He is the joker." Do not let yourself be defined by negative, superficial terms. These kinds of descriptions are at best incomplete, but they reveal how people think about others on a very basic level. There is something about every individual that others easily identify them with. Some examples of this cannot be helped, like your age or gender, but other aspects are within your control. Make sure that your behavior gives you the highest reputation possible. Your reputation is associated with your defining characteristics. Do not be the monkey in the room whose purpose appears to be the entertainment of others. Frequently telling jokes may make you welcome company, but only for amusement, not for your virtues or practical abilities.

Honor Your Uniqueness and Be Creative

None of this means that you should become a conformist or copy others to avoid social marginalization. It is false and misleading to suggest that you should necessarily emulate someone else. The situations and personal qualities that helped someone else attain their objectives were unique to one specific time, place, and individual—never to be repeated precisely again. If Napoleon or Churchill had lived in times of peace they probably would not have had the opportunity to become great. Do not assume that because someone is famous or rich you can become like them if you just do what they did. You too are unique and have a specific niche in time. Instead of being a follower, you must assimilate the wisdom of others without expecting it to work like a formula. While there are no exact recurrences in history, there are consistent themes that are predictable enough for you to antic-ipate. Developing an effective strategy involves understanding the tendencies others have to behave in a way you can anticipate and then acting or responding in a way that maximizes a desired outcome. Do not be lured into thinking that just because someone is famous or admired they know the path to personal achievement. There are many such individuals who attained their success with little effort because of the talents they were born with: good fortune, a family name, or an inheritance. But history is also filled with accounts of success for those who had none of these resources or blessings.

Admire, But Do Not Mimic Your Heroes

Success is not derived from mimicry—even mimicry of the great. The time, situation, and people involved when someone else became successful will never repeat themselves exactly. Look around and you will see that in the world today there are millions of clever, ambitious individuals striving for success who believe that by copying someone else or by using a formula they will be able to repeat the successes of others who came before them. But this is usually a fiction. Most will remain mediocre because there is no one strategy that produces the same outcomes every time. Your idols should inspire you—perhaps in countless ways—but you can never be just like them. They distinguished themselves with originality and innovation and took calculated risks. Learn from others, experiment with the wisdom, but honor your own uniqueness and the peculiarities of your surroundings.

Be a Person of Your Times

It is critical to be a person of your times. What "worked" socially even two decades ago is not necessarily what works now. If you want to maximize your appeal to others, you must embrace the spirit of the age. *Be a person of your times.* In our age, it is fashionable to be casual, approachable, and plain speaking, regardless of social status. Times have changed: patrician eloquence creates distance from others and is usually perceived as an attempt to act superior. People who interact with the public at large and within a circle of experts provide excellent examples of how to communicate. It is common for experts in their fields to have blogs that describe their work in layman's terms, even though in other venues they use more sophisticated language when communicating with their peers.

Today, the higher and the lower classes of society pretend that they are on the same level. Those with esteemed reputations want to pass the test of humility while the rest of us seek to have our opinions respectfully acknowledged by them. But making everything a democratic affectation does not change the fact that some people within the herd of humanity have abilities or resources that others do not. Therefore, those with talents must occasionally show themselves above the norm by a word or action which demonstrates ability. For the most part it is best to blend in to your social environment, but find a way to stand out a little bit—but not too much—so that you are not forgotten and to ensure that your talents and abilities can be recognized.

Despite the fact that people are impressed by superficial things, when you do communicate, do so clearly. The purpose of language is to communicate. If your language is above the level of the person you are talking with, then you are failing at your purpose. But do not "dumb down" what you have to say by appealing to the lowest type of speech. Who is your audience? Do not be like the selfish person who uses communication merely to impress others. It is better to aim for the good that can be done rather than to seek self-glorification. However, people can become offended if they think you are dumbing things down too much. If you are an expert in something speaking to laymen, sprinkle your words with a clever turn of phrase or technical term just enough to remind them that you are at a higher level in your area of expertise. This approach will also pique intrigue and interest.

Final Note: What's in a Name?

An example of something "superficial" is the impact of a person's birth name on his or her psyche over time. On the one hand, a name is a superficial thing; after all, by itself it says nothing about someone. Shouldn't someone's character, skills, and personality and a hundred other things be more important than a mere name? On the other hand, a name is the most important word associated with you that—like it or not—has impacted how others treated you, especially during your most formative childhood years. Our identity is partly shaped by the way we are treated by other people—a concept psychologists call the *looking-glass self*. Certain names make us more vulnerable to scrutiny while other names conform to societal norms. How others respond to our name has a psychological impact. If others do not respond positively to a name, a person is not likely to like their own name. These perceptions affect an individual's self-esteem.

There are many studies correlating names with career and academic success. Men with shorter first names are overrepresented as CEOs of successful companies. Women at the top of corporations are more likely to use their full names and middle initials. Those with shorter names, starting closer to the beginning of the alphabet, and easy to pronounce, statistically tend to be more successful. On the other hand, individuals with certain names are at a disadvantage. (Remember the Johnny Cash song about a boy named Sue who gets in a fight with his father who named him!) Individuals with offbeat names may be continually teased in school, which in turn damages their self-image and can then have lasting psychological effects. Boys with feminine-sounding names are more likely to have behavioral problems and get suspended from school. There is also the issue of economic and racial discrimination. In England, those with lower-class names are viewed with bias; in the USA, people with names associated with certain racial minorities are less likely to get interviewed and hired.

"Should I change my name?" Not necessarily. Correlation does not equal causation. There are thousands of people with the "worst" names doing well while thousands more with preferred names struggle. Therefore changing one's name does not guarantee anything. Right now, if you are reading this you are most likely already an adult with an established life and mindset. On the other hand, if you do not like your name or want to convey a certain impression, it could be beneficial to change your name or perhaps use a nickname that you are more comfortable about using—especially if you are planning a major life or career change.

Taking Inventory

Ask yourself…

- Are you easily swayed by appearances?
- Are you susceptible to the seduction of superficial charms?
- Do you confuse authenticity with affectations like mannerisms, clothing, and style?

Change Something

Do things differently…

- Get rid of bad habits and superficial traits that get in the way of your success.

- Look beyond obvious words and actions to discern the reality of a situation.
- Accept that selfishness can trump even sincere sympathy, forgiveness, and other desirable qualities.

Develop Wisdom

Consider that...

- It is necessary to distinguish between appearances and reality.
- Recognize that wisdom is more valuable and advantageous in the long run than superficially pleasing qualities.

Chapter 6

Law 6: Boldness and Audacity Produce Success

Never was anything great achieved without danger.
—Niccolò Machiavelli

A majority of individuals are predictable, dislike change, and view life through the prism of very narrow self-interests. When you act boldly, decisively, and swiftly, you create surprise and respect from others. But bold actions usually involve risk and should be the exception, not the rule. There are key times when unpredictable boldness is required for success. At other times it is a preference based on your tolerance for risk.

Boldness does not mean rashness—acting impulsively. Instead, it is an intelligent tactic that involves a) acting in a way that seems unpredictable to others, b) executing a plan quickly and confidently, and c) accepting a level of risk beforehand in order to not hesitate during execution. Boldness requires courage and there are no guarantees, but it can produce wonderful results and serve you across a wide variety of circumstances.

A Crisis Requires a Bold Response

Timely action is called for during a crisis. When sudden, unpredictable events occur, you hesitate to your own peril. Careful deliberation and cautiousness have their place, but they are luxuries that you cannot always afford. Generally speaking, a crisis consists of a threatening problem combined with a short response time; the longer you delay responding, the more the crisis will grow. Act quickly to subdue a growing menace. Some problems are analogous to infections; they can spread quickly and have dire consequences. Examples of crises include a sudden failure of magnitude, escalating interpersonal attacks, and the surprise intervention of some unexpected external force. When you notice an emerging crisis, be quick, but not too quick, to respond. Your response should always be preceded by timely rational thinking. Rash, ill-thought-out responses, such as those motivated by panic or anger, will exacerbate problems or even create new ones. Identify the variables, assess your options, and respond decisively. Aim for ending quickly what has gotten out of hand.

There are times when a sudden event induces panic or confusion in others. If you are always looking ahead and thinking of the optimal response in a worse-case scenario, then you will be much more prepared than others. Considering hypothetical situations reduces the risk of getting blindsided and disoriented. You will have some idea of what you are going to do, which saves time when the moment of crisis arrives. Of course it can be impossible to know exactly what to do during a crisis, but at the very least, considering possible scenarios sometimes help identify what *not* to do, shortening your response time. If you have a desire to make an impression upon others, use a crisis to your benefit. People are often desperate for a leader to save them when they feel scared or threatened. In the end, those who take charge effectively rather than becoming paralyzed with indecision end up gaining respect from others.

Accept Risk When There Is Little to Lose

At key times, quick action is called for when you can gain much, but lose little or nothing at all. For example, many people have simply asked for something, expecting to be turned down, but were not. Only laziness or fear of failure prevents making small efforts that could pay off in big ways. But do not be like the gambler who repeats risk over and over, only to cumulatively lose too much. Avoid appearing the opportunist by carefully choosing what risks to take. If a small effort comes to nothing, then what have you lost? But on a rare occasion a small effort can either prevent calamity or produce a victory. There are many people who have had doors of opportunity open for them simply because they did something simple, obvious, or easy.

A Prevention Focus Is Contrary to Boldness

One mistake people make is that they are overly *prevention focused*. They live in fear, scared of losing what they have, and use the majority of their time and energy trying to stay safe, avoid problems, and get along with everyone. This is like going to battle with a shield but without a sword. Such individuals tend to build walls to protect themselves from any form of loss— financial, social, or professional. Sure, keeping all one's money in the bank might be safest, but is it going to maximize your net worth? Avoiding social risk might protect you from rejection, but what about a stagnant social life? Bunkering down in a "safe" job might provide security, but what opportunities are you missing?

The safe path is seldom the path of greatness. It is better to blend caution with the "sword" of a *promotion focus*. This involves a willingness to take risks, seek out opportunities, and maximize one's potential. Teddy Roosevelt once said, "Nothing good in life happens without risk." Creativity and innovation can produce fantastic results, but not without the possibility of failure. Make it a habit to look for opportunities that require calculated risks.

Execute Plans During Changing Times

During times of changing circumstances people become apprehensive and fearful, wondering how everything will turn out. Be ready during these times to implement your own plans that would otherwise become a focus of criticism. The winds of change will preoccupy others and distract attention away from your designs. Look for the most decisive moment to act for the greatest results.

Real-life example

Roberto wanted to restructure the human resources department in some big ways. He was worried that if he tried to execute his plans, one of the corporate attorneys might insist upon scrutinizing everything, possibly delaying the process by months. As he pondered what to do, he learned that their mutual employer had suddenly gotten hit with three lawsuits. In response, all of the attorneys became overwhelmed and preoccupied with new work. Roberto decided that now was the time to implement his plans. He executed his plans and no one from the legal team had the time or opportunity to derail his efforts.

Use Bold Actions to Buy Time When Weakened

Selfish and antagonistic people almost never take on their equals or those stronger than them unless necessary. Instead, they opportunistically prey on the weak. Unfortunately, each of us at some point will experience a point in time where, for whatever reason, we are weakened, perhaps by stress, physical illness, or a big problem that takes up a lot of time and energy. At such times, cut-throat opportunists may perceive your weakness as something to exploit. When you are weakened, and unable to be at your best, a bold act, done with confidence, will for at least a brief time make others stop and wait to see whether you are truly weak or merely appeared to be weak. Be like the wounded lion that suddenly sits up and roars, momentarily making the hyenas step back in fear. Such bold acts buy time—a precious commodity.

The opposite tactic can also be useful: purposefully feigning weakness serves as a lure to selfish and antagonistic people. As they circle a potential victim to exploit, they get too comfortable, feeling like they are in a dominant position when they are not. This makes them vulnerable to mistakes such as executing plans prematurely or revealing their true feelings about a person; when you suddenly snap back to normal, your opponents will be caught off-guard.

Boldly Intervene to Tip the Scales in Conflict

When people are engaged in conflict the typical response of observers is to "stay out of it." After all, why take on troubles that are not your own? This is wise sometimes, but not all of the time. Think about warfare analogies. When two nations are at war, and evenly matched, a third nation that enters the conflict could easily tip the scales and produce a desired outcome. It is no different within small, competing groups or even disputes between individuals. When there is conflict between other parties, ask yourself whether it is in your interest for one side to win over the other. Decide whether entering the conflict to help one side win is worth it to you. Such executions should be decisive, not half-hearted. Make sure that there is a good reason to enter a conflict in order to avoid being perceived as opportunistic.

Concentrate Your Resources

When you intensely desire to accomplish one goal in particular, it may be necessary to let other things go and solely devote yourself to the task. Many artists and writers have been very successful by "ignoring the world" and assiduously devoting themselves to particular projects. This is a form of boldness insofar as it involves acting contrary to the norm and concentrating one's efforts. It is analogous to certain concentrations of strength in warfare. A small number of organized soldiers, for example, can rout a much larger unorganized force or even control an entire population. The same number of soldiers, spread out too thinly, would not be strong enough to use their force effectively. Concentrating resources is also useful for organizations, like businesses and institutions. For example, it might be better to focus on marketing one product rather than several; it might be better to have a small, highly skilled team working together rather than separated into smaller groups.

But concentration is not enough: discipline is required. Just as a concentration of soldiers would not be effective without coordination, each aspect of us as individuals—our emotions, thoughts, and actions—should be in sync when executing a task. The alternative is unacceptable: to rely on luck or charity to achieve a goal. Do not be like the type of person who is always scheming to achieve something by getting lucky or peddling some gimmick. While occasionally a schemer gets lucky, in most cases they have nothing to show for their efforts. There is nothing more powerful than concentrated efforts combined with discipline—nothing!

Boldly Roll with Criticism to Baffle Your Opponent

Clever manipulators and exploiters are good at finding ways to be critical or accusatory without appearing to break any social rules. These "attacks" are expected to provoke a reaction of distress that causes the targeted person to react in a submissive manner. As noted earlier, the motive is usually a selfish, hidden agenda of some kind. You can frustrate their accusations by faking a naïve trust in what they are saying and interpreting their language literally. In doing so, you surprise and baffle your opponent who expects a completely different reaction. Consider the following scenario:

> *Jason was a supervising broker for a large financial firm. He viewed Kathy, another supervisor, as competition for an executive position. He made many attempts to undermine and demoralize her, but nothing he did worked. Every time he criticized her decisions, instead of getting angry, Kathy seemed grateful and even enthusiastic. Whenever his complaints were specific, she responded by saying that his concern was so critical and important that she would make sure no one else made the same mistake by writing changes into policy for her department. She said that she would let*

the executive team know about his criticisms, adding that hopefully all the brokers would need to comply with them.

She also insisted that given the many issues he raised about her, she would be sure to repeat them to the executive every single time to confirm that she was responding correctly. She invited him to discuss his concerns about her with the executive team. She added that she knew that he was "just trying to help" and said she would seek approval to have more meetings to discuss his criticisms that could help her team.

Jason feared that his numerous complaints about Kathy would make him appear petty if she repeatedly reported them to the executives. Moreover, he did not like the idea of taking up his time with more meetings or making everything into a company policy. Jason decided that criticizing Kathy was more trouble than it was worth, and besides, she seemed completely oblivious to his attempt to unsettle her.

In the above example Kathy did not act as expected. She embraced Jason's criticisms, which seemed to him like arrows harmlessly passing through her body. Of course there are many situations where this tactic would not work. For example, it would not be appropriate to "roll" with total lies or scandalous allegations. There are times when you must overtly counter-attack, but the easier path is to win with cleverness. Retaliating, appealing for mercy, or arguing can be self-defeating because these responses indicate that you are taking attacks seriously, which leads others to wonder whether there is credibility to your opponent's claims.

By responding with naïve acceptance you are following the wisdom of certain Eastern philosophies which teach that you can win by using your challenger's own energy against him. A side benefit of this approach is that you remain blameless because you are only taking a person at his or her word. This can be protective if your opponent ends up sticking around a while. It is harder to hold a grudge against someone who always appeared to do the right thing. This tactic works best when you appear completely sincere in your efforts. If your opponent can tell that you are merely acting, he or she might call your bluff.

Act Boldly When It Is Necessary to Cause Pain

Sometimes in order to carry out a plan we must act in a way opposed by others. Announcing a divorce, firing an employee, or preventing someone from getting what they want can be necessary actions. At such times, commit to following through. Announce your decision confidently and decisively. Hesitation will be interpreted as self-doubt. Do not apologize for your actions—if you do, no one will appreciate it because they perceive themselves as victims. Do not act timidly or second-guess yourself which opens the door for others to pleading, negotiating, and arguing—when such interactions fail, resentments double.

Pay Attention to Streaks

Boldness should involve good timing. Pay attention to luck without becoming superstitious. There are times in life when things have a pattern of going better or worse. Sometimes we know the reason; sometimes it remains hidden. When things seem to be going poorly, bunker down into caution; act more slowly and do not take risks. Wait for the cloudy storm to eventually pass. When there seems to be a pattern of success, "strike while the iron is hot"; act with greater confidence—not carelessly, but with forethought. Go in the direction that the universe seems to encourage. There are those who were unlucky in one time or place, but found success in another.

Manage Blunders with Preparation and Deflection

Given enough time, even the most brilliant and moral individuals commit serious mistakes. Be aware that your mistakes are ammunition that your competitors could use against you; some might gladly criticize or mock you in the hope that you will become demoralized and ultimately fail in your endeavors. Those above you in authority might question your judgment or lose confidence in your abilities. If you have followers, they might abandon you if they think they are on a sinking ship. Your competitors will be eager to replace you. In extreme cases a substantial blunder might result in total disaster. Knowing that you could lose everything means that you have the advantage of preparing for it. The following describes three preparation methods to avoid mistakes.

Preparation tactic # 1: Build up credit

Have you ever noticed that some individuals are able to bounce back from catastrophe while others are obliterated by it? The best preventative measure is to build up what psychologists call *idiosyncrasy credits*. Having a long record of maintaining a favorable reputation, competence, and solid support among your peers or the community can act as a buffer against crises. Like a car that takes a beating but keeps going, a very positive reputation is a protective factor. In some instances, it is possible for someone to achieve such high social regard that he or she is insulated from damage from virtually everything except extreme acts of moral turpitude. This ascendant status is rare and requires that someone have significant positive credit to the extent that even a major blow can be withstood. This phenomenon is the reason that history is replete with stories of popular figures with damaged reputations who managed to regain their status—although not always to the same degree.

Preparation tactic # 2: Collect ammunition, but keep your hands clean

The power of accusations is great. Anyone at any time can accuse you of something, automatically leading others to wonder if it is true. This puts you on the defensive—a weak position. If you suspect that someone could at some point make allegations against you, prepare by secretly logging evidence that could be used against that person if necessary. For example, when someone sends you a politically incorrect email—perhaps making fun of someone, criticizing a superior, or using racial slurs—without telling anyone, collect those emails. Suppose someone complains a lot or makes accusations against others—keep copies of those communications for future use. Later, if the author of these kinds of communications falsely accuses you of something, you have two ways to counter-attack: a) by explaining that if they do not retract their allegations you can show others these indiscretions, or b) disclosing these communications to others to undermine their credibility.

Do not wait for months or years to go by to track down those emails, texts, or voicemails that could protect you. Instead, have them ready at hand to be used as needed. If they are never needed, you can always delete them. Do not underestimate how many brief, negative communications can make someone look badly when viewed side-by-side. But be careful to only make use of such information during a crisis. When others discover that you are a "collector" of indiscretions, they will become suspicious and wary of your presence. After all, most people (at least rarely) communicate something inappropriate. It might be better to let others know that you only recently decided to go back and look at old emails or other communications rather than admitting that you collected them for a long period of time.

The following are two examples of how this effort can be helpful:

Example A

Dan, you have threatened to make false accusations against me, but if you do, I will show others the stack of emails I have from you over the last three years where you made over 30 accusations about me, used profanities, and referred to the CEO as an "asshole."

Example B

Yes, I know Dan has accused me of a serious indiscretion. I plan to show at the HR meeting proof that he has not only falsely accused people of many things over the years, but has made insulting statements about management.

The above tactic can be very powerful. Few people are mindful of the cumulative impact of little indiscretions over a long period of time. If someone sent an email calling the CEO a "bitch," after a few days without any negative reaction they are likely to think that they are safe from criticism.

Make note of the power of reversal: anything you communicate can be used against you. Make sure that you keep your hands clean by not creating a record of indiscretions. If you need to communicate something risky, do so with personal, oral communications. Someone's memory of a conversation can always be doubted, but records and electronic communications cannot.

Preparation tactic # 3: Make the correctable mistake

Problems that can be managed are more desirable than problems that cannot. If you have to choose between two or more risky alternatives, pick the option that—if it fails—you are mostly likely to be able to fix or that will cause the least damage. Try to ensure that as few people as possible will notice your mistakes. If possible, choose conditions that you can quickly enter and exit. Test an idea or plan within a small, controlled environment or by getting feedback from a small number of people. If you notice your plans starting to fail, shut them down quickly.

Skillfully Respond to Allegations

Allegations can be true or false, but in either case a swift defense is needed. Act too slowly and—like a fire—rumors and biases against you build up, undermining your defense before you have even begun. Even when you have done something wrong, if you do not skillfully respond the "fire" of your difficulties will grow beyond what you deserve. Whether innocent, guilty, or somewhere in between, do not cave in to pressure without considering all your options. The responses described below are critical to consider in such circumstances.

First response: Deny the allegations

If the allegations are false, deny them entirely. But what if the accusations are accurate or partly accurate? A responsible person still needs to defend themselves. After all, even true accusations can be made with malicious motivations. At times it is necessary to stonewall accusations, even if they are accurate, by insisting upon 100% accuracy. Demand all of the facts and definitions of terms. Someone accused of "dishonesty" could respond by demanding to know exactly when this supposedly occurred, who was there, what was allegedly said, proof of these things, and what exactly "dishonest" is supposed to mean. None of this involves denying any wrongdoing, but it slows things down and ensures that you do not admit to one tidbit more of an error than actually did occur.

Second response: Justifiably externalize blame

Few are the times in life when someone makes serious mistakes without external influences. Make the case that your mistake was partly due to abnormal circumstances. Identify and point out any mitigating factors. Examples of this include unreasonable timelines, distractions, interferences, inaccurate information, and bad advice. A version of externalizing blame is to accept *partial* responsibility for a mistake. If someone else is to blame, partly or fully, then make it known. Unless you find yourself in some untouchable position, do not "take one for the team." It might be appreciated at first, but it is you who has to live with the stigma and you cannot count on others doing the same for you in the future.

Third response: Surrender and apologize

If you have made a huge, obvious, undeniable blunder, carefully assess the situation. The worst-case scenario is that the tactics described above are inapplicable or ineffective. As counter-intuitive as it sounds, such a situation requires that you surrender: openly admit your error and take full responsibility. This serves two strategic purposes. First, it neutralizes your accusers—accusations are most powerful when someone denies them. (There might be some residual scorn, but this tends to quickly fade away.) Second, by surrendering you are no longer in the undesirable position of defending yourself, which is a position of weakness. Third, full disclosure means that you have no further need to apologize—another weak position. The surrender strategy requires consistency: do not respond to counter-attacks or emotional provocations intended to provoke a reaction. You might even benefit from using a modicum of humor to demonstrate to others that you have not been entirely thrown off course by your error, e.g. "Man, I really screwed up. Even my dog hates me now."

Thankfully, there are still many people in the world who respect an honest confession over continued denial. Some will appreciate your bold honesty. But do not think that due to support or a great reputation you can avoid surrendering to extremely damaging, proven, obvious allegations. If you do not surrender in such cases, others will perceive you to be arrogant and think that you believe that you are above the rules that everyone else has to follow. Many great historical figures have used the surrender tactic. Maybe you do not have the clout of such individuals, but neither do you have the magnitude of their problems.

Taking Inventory

Ask yourself...

- Are you afraid of taking risks or making bold decisions?
- Do you know how to take advantage of crises, conflict, and change?
- Have you considered methods to best manage mistakes and accusations?

Change Something

Do things differently...

- Take advantage of opportunities by acting unpredictably.
- Execute your plans with good timing.
- Impress others with bold moves.
- Protect yourself by possessing a good reputation and a clean record.

Develop Wisdom

- Look for opportunities and strike while the iron is hot.
- Understand that most people are not bold and do not like risks, but they can be impressed by those who act outside the box.
- Be humble and as a last resort fully admit and accept serious mistakes.

Chapter 7

Law 7: Conflict Is Inevitable and Selectively Advantageous

Life is a warfare against the malice of others.
—Baltasar Gracián

There is no need to seek out conflict—it will come to you. All social interactions are potential conflicts. Any idea, opinion, topic, preference, circumstance or plan can become a source of conflict. Conflict is inevitable; therefore, knowing how to deal with it is more important than knowing how to avoid it. Mastering conflict is not easy, but the payoff can be huge: it can greatly increase self-confidence and expedite solutions to a multitude of problems over time. Conflict should not always be dreaded; it can open up many doors of opportunity that otherwise remain shut. Many people avoid conflict because they find it too stressful to capitalize on opportunities. Unfortunately, when people of integrity refuse to engage in conflict, the strong and selfish respond by acting assertively to get what they want. Chronic avoiders of conflict find themselves manipulated and dominated by others. On the other hand, those with positive intentions who master the art of conflict can learn to win and use their success to do a tremendous amount of good for themselves and others.

Embrace Conflict

Those who value peace and a calm mind should not always avoid conflict. *As counter-intuitive as it sounds, the study of conflict is most necessary for those who desire the absence of conflict.* Passive or hesitant responses convey the impression of weakness and allow aggressively selfish individuals greater control of resources. For this reason, there are more dangers in avoiding conflict than skillfully engaging it. No matter how much you prefer social harmony and peace of mind over conflict, there are times when action is needed, either now or later.

Do not be afraid of conflict—embrace it. Conflict works because it results in change and the winner can ensure that it is a change for the better. Even when you lose, you sometimes end up with concessions and compromises not otherwise gotten. Rolling over and letting others take control undermines not only your success, but your dignity. Conflict is like a fork in the road that forces us to decide which direction to take; what decision to make; what person to utilize; and what needs to happen next. No one should be expected to like conflict, but an overly negative attitude will drain the willpower and resolve needed to take on necessary challenges.

Two Types of Conflict

Conflict involves two parties opposing each other in some way, usually with underlying negative feelings such as resentment or anger. There are two broad categories of conflict. On the positive side, there is *constructive conflict*. This occurs when there is hope for a win-win scenario by both parties. Both sides aim to be objective, respectful, and do not violate each other's rights. There are positive intentions, but different opinions. Communication tends to be give-and-take and compromise is on the table. Things are not taken personally. Criticism is well-intentioned. Constructive conflict is the easiest form of conflict to manage.

Destructive conflict occurs when a disagreement is costly to you and someone else. Be alert for indications of mutually destructive conflict that are likely to intensify into personal attacks or a crisis. Conversations that begin with criticism can escalate into a pattern of blame, counter-blame, and entrenched defensiveness. Antagonistic individuals tend to begin conversations with a harsh criticism to assert their dominance or intimidate others; in response, the other person either caves in to their demands or quickly feels defensive and provoked to anger. If you give in to an emotional, defensive response, you become trapped in a power struggle that has little to do with the "facts" about a problem. A difference of opinion is one kind of problem, but taking things personally is a second kind of problem, sabotaging efforts to accomplish anything at all.

Characteristics of destructive conflict:

1) Your opponent makes harsh or judgmental statements about you personally.
2) There is no room for compromise, i.e. you are "wrong" no matter what.
3) There is an attempt to control you rather than solve the problem.
4) Your opponent is not straightforward about a deeper issue bothering him or her.
5) You are talked down to as being inferior.
6) There is an emerging pattern of escalation, such as personal criticisms, derogatory language, or intimidating behavior.
7) False accusations are made.
8) There are attempts to exploit your weaknesses.
9) There is reason to believe that the conflict is driven by an undisclosed, hidden agenda.
10) Attempts are made to rally others against you.

Destructive conflict is much harder to manage than constructive conflict. The focus of this chapter is exclusively upon destructive conflict. This type of conflict is usually emotionally unsettling and accompanied by a high level of stress. The following addresses how to engage destructive conflict by utilizing several broad approaches; the first of these includes preparation, determining the self-interested motive, and strategy development.

Preparation: Get Information

The first step prior to engaging conflict is to obtain as much information as possible. Find out everything you can about the nature of the problem and the players involved. Become an "expert" about the situation. Try to perceive the conflict from the point of view of others to determine what it might take to win them to your side. If a particular person is a source of conflict, learn about their personality, history, circumstances, strengths and weaknesses. Learn about the nuts and bolts of the situation. Collecting objective sources of facts, such as from documents, preferably linked to names and dates, can be indispensable. If at some future point you need to argue your case, have the answers ready ahead of time. Responding "I don't know" will only make others wonder why you did not do your homework if you really cared about an issue.

Determine the Self-Interested Motive

As discussed in Chapter 1, self-interest is the primary motivation for human behavior. This observation is especially relevant to interpersonal conflict involving two or more strong, opposing preferences and opinions. *The primary reason for all conflict is competing self-interest.* If one person or group has different self-interested motives than the other party, conflict is likely to occur. This is especially true when concealed, selfish motivations are present. Motives that are not prosocial are not likely to be discussed, limiting dialogue that could lead to conflict resolution. A self-interested point of view can be identified as selfish when there is little concern for anyone else and someone is willing to violate the rights of others to get their way. Selfishness is most likely to develop into destructive conflict. There are three possible roots of destructive conflict: the known, the concealed, and a combination of both.

Explicit reasons for conflict

The explicit reason is whatever has been identified by both parties as the basis for the conflict, e.g. "We cannot agree on the timing to move forward with our plan." The explicit reason usually includes disagreements about goals, priorities, timing, or the use of resources. Most people will give prosocial reasons for pushing a certain agenda, for example, "I just want to raise our children right," or "I want our small business to grow." Other examples include how to improve efficiency, solve a problem, increase teamwork, etc. Conflicts between couples are most often about issues like money, sex, raising children, commitment, sharing responsibilities, and communication.

The issues identified in explicit conflict should appear to be the focus, even if you have other, underlying positive motivations. It would not make sense to say out loud, "I know profits would be huge, but I oppose the investment because of my personal values." Values-based motivations should usually be kept to oneself; otherwise, they will be dismissed by others as a personal bias that should not be part of the equation. Values are personally important, but within organizations economic or practical arguments tend to have more merit.

Concealed reasons for conflict

Few people ever admit personal motivations that are not considered prosocial or that would reflect poorly on them. Beneath a socially acceptable veneer, many are motivated by greed or power. It is therefore up to you to make your best guess as to whether such underlying motivations exist. Look for hints — a word here or there might seem innocent, but if you add them up do you see a pattern? What emotional reactions have you noticed? Has your opponent ever made a mistake and let slip, even one time, a hidden motivation? Above all, contemplate the question, "If my opponent got his way, how would he or she benefit?"

If your opponent has a concealed agenda, they will go to great lengths to keep it that way. Discovering a concealed, selfish agenda is ammunition in your pocket. For example, "Kim's idea to contract with a vendor was shot down after people learned that he had just bought a lot of stock in the company." This also holds true for personal relationships, e.g. "Mandy said she wanted custody of their daughter because she was the best parent, but one of her emails said she only wanted custody for the sake of alimony."

After you identify a concealed agenda, do not call attention to it unless you have evidence. It does not matter whether you "know" someone has a concealed agenda; without evidence, your opponent can call you a false accuser, thereby undermining your credibility. If it helps, imagine presenting the evidence in court. Could you make a case?

Know Thyself

While understanding your own motivations and those of others is critical to managing conflict, it is also necessary to manage emotions. Emotional extremes such as intense anger or anxiety will be viewed by others as weaknesses. Consider your own typical feelings and reactions when engaging in conflict. The way most people respond to conflict has a lot to do with their family of origin. How was conflict dealt with in your family before you became an adult? If your family discouraged the expression of opinions or feelings, then you might be prone to conflict-avoidance or anxiety. Individuals from aggressive families have an entirely different set of problems. In some families it is "normal" to deal with conflict by arguing loudly and displaying strong emotion. Later in life, people from such families are prone to displaying intense reactions that appear to others to be over-the-top. They can be controlling or brutally honest, hurting the feelings of others, who view them as threatening.

There are of course families where conflict is managed in a healthy manner. A healthy assertiveness is modeled to children by parents who try to express themselves and negotiate conflict without fear, suppression, or intense anger. But whether you come from a family that was conflict-avoidant, aggressive, or healthy, you are now a mature adult and responsible for understanding how your past experiences have influenced your style. This understanding will help you to put a check on unwanted automatic responses. Beyond your self-knowledge, understanding someone else's proclivities might be helpful as well. Prior to entering a conflicted situation, ask yourself the following questions:

How does someone's personal history influence their style of dealing with conflict?
Is there a tendency to avoid problems?
Is there a tendency to be aggressive toward others?
Is someone's attitude toward conflict an extreme of some kind, such as "Fight back" or "Avoid rocking the boat"?
Does someone prefer conflict over social harmony?

Assess Your Position

Obviously it would be foolish to respond to those above you in the same manner as a colleague or friend. How you respond to conflict should be according to your level of power, which is the ability to control or influence others. Assess your position in three ways: your relationship with the person; the resources each of you has control over, and the authority to force action.

When in conflict, identify and place yourself in one of the following four categories:

High power / low power: This is where you are clearly in the dominant position.
Low power / high power: This is where you are in a weak

position in terms of resources and/or authority. For example, if the person you are having conflict with can cause personal or professional loss.

Equal power: Where you and the other person have equivalent positions.

Mixed power: This form of power is an unequal mix of authority and resources. For example, when person A has a higher position of authority than person B, but person B has more valuable resources such as highly sought technical skills, better connections, or some irreplaceable quality. Make a distinction between overt power and subtle power. Usually these two coincide, but not always. For example, a skilled surgeon might not have any administrative authority but makes the hospital so much money that he or she always seems to get their way. Another example would be a low-level employee that might not have much authority but is nonetheless socially influential due to his or her personal connections.

Obviously those with more power over you have the greatest advantage in conflict. Adjust your tactics and responses to conflict according to your position in relation to another person. Do not assume that someone in a lower power position than you will be easy to best in conflict. Sometimes the most clever and prudent individuals have low power; sometimes those with low power today gain power over time.

Remain Blameless

Destructive conflict can be highly distressing. When conflict seems to be escalating, you cannot win by using tactics that reflect poorly upon you or that could result in negative consequences. If you are seen as doing something antisocial, it could be used against you, regardless of whether your opponent has also done wrong. Therefore, you must respond to destructive conflict subtly, without any evidence of wrongdoing. Some people are blindsided by conflict and need time to think before responding. The easiest way to remain blameless is to think before you speak, stick to the facts, and control your emotions.

Think before you speak

In the midst of conflict, anything you say could be used against you. As a precaution, before you speak, imagine that everything you say is going to be on a transcript and read by others. How would it be received? Be careful with your words so they do not become ammunition for others to use against you. Be succinct and do not ramble on and on. Given a choice, it is better to be silent than to carelessly say many words.

Communicate with subtle grace

Anything that you would like to say can be communicated subtly. If you are unsure how to phrase something, put it in the form of a question. For example, instead of saying, "You have an agenda to make me miserable so that I quit and you can take over!" say, "Do you want me to stay at this company? Maybe it's not true. I would like to know." These "I" statements, combined with questions, make someone appear totally blameless, but with the right tone and timing someone will get the message that you are on to their agenda. With enough forethought, you can always find a blameless way to say what is really on your mind in a way that would pass social scrutiny. Self-effacing speculation is another blameless way to communicate, e.g. "I'm not sure, but is it possible that Becky started these rumors? I hope not. I could be totally in left field." Others will get the real message you are sending, but in the process you are immune from prosecution.

Stick to the facts

State the facts about a conflict as objectively as you can, for example, "The job was not done" rather than "You are lazy."

After you have pointed out the problem—not the person—ask for some kind of *specific* change. If you have made mistakes or bear responsibility for something, admit it, e.g. "I did make a mistake." Once you openly admit something, accusations lose their power. Verbally attacking someone, criticizing, blaming, or using judgmental language will provoke hostile reactions and make you appear antagonistic. On the other hand, no one can credibly deny facts.

Control your emotions and resist impulsive responses

During times of conflict, stress levels increase and emotions intensify. If you give in to impulsive responses, like anger or sarcasm, it might be used against you in the future. Slow down, think, and imagine how what you do or say will be received by others. There is nothing wrong with internally being angry or distressed, but do not let strong feelings drive your behavior or decision-making process. If you "take the high road," but the other person loses emotional control, you will seem like the reasonable party by comparison.

At Key Times, Provoke Conflict

Conflict is sometimes predictable. If you sense it is coming, do not always patiently wait for it to happen; make it happen on your own terms. When you provoke inevitable conflict, you get the huge advantages of preparing and choosing the place and time. With antagonistic personalities, procrastination and appeasement merely postpone conflict, but seldom prevent it. When conflict is inevitable, it is better to engage in it sooner rather than later. Take advantage of circumstances where the antagonistic are at their weakest. For example, perhaps someone is temporarily under high levels of stress—that might be the time to engage them. Antagonistic personalities tend to perform more poorly under stress and succumb to emotional reactions, resulting in mistakes that can be used to your advantage. This may not sound very kind, but remember that it is specific to highly selfish individuals who have targeted you with antagonism.

Revenge Is More Trouble Than It Is Worth

When someone is selfish, will giving someone a taste of their own medicine put an end to bad behavior? If you get back at someone, won't he or she know how badly it felt and stop treating you that way? While it might seem natural to figuratively (or literally) want to "hit someone who hits you," this tit-for-tat response is highly risky. Repaying harm with harm can lead to resentment and escalation of conflict. On the other hand, you cannot be passive, either, or you might end up being someone's punching-bag.

Usually the goal of revenge is threefold: 1) to get the person to hurt as much as you did, 2) to get them to feel genuine remorse because their pain will help them understand how much they hurt you, and 3) that this genuine remorse will cause them never to hurt you in the same way again. Sometimes we hope the pain and suffering they feel will reform their character by creating empathy. But these hopes are false. *Revenge almost never proves effective.* Why does revenge not work? First, it can lead to escalating aggression as each person takes turns "getting back" at the other. Eventually, the escalation can get to an out-of-control point where there are concerns about litigation, destruction of reputation, or even violence. Second, since no one respects vengeful behavior, once it is discovered, no one looks good, and within a family or organization it can impact your reputation or lead to disciplinary action. Third, even when there is a "winner," the lingering resentment will leave the "loser" looking for any window of opportunity for retaliation. If the emotional wound is too deep, it may never heal. Finally, if one or more persons in the relationship are extremely dysfunctional or have nothing to lose, no amount of suffering will stop their bad behavior.

Personal Relationships and Conflict

Not long ago, one of the more difficult items on a standardized IQ test included the question, "What do an enemy and friend have in common?" The answer was "a relationship." While it is easy to think of enemies as having nothing in common because they are at war with each other, in actuality it is the very nature of the conflict that they have in common. They share negative emotions toward each other, have similar objectives, and devote their energies against each other, interacting accordingly. In many instances the parties involved in conflict have a lot in common. This is especially true when conflict happens in the aftermath of a failed personal relationship, such as a divorce. Lingering emotions can complicate how to respond strategically. The worst kinds of conflict occur when someone was close to another person. There are many people in this world who hate a parent, former friend, or ex-spouse, but only because their attempts at love failed—not because they no longer care. When someone loves something or someone, but it escapes them, resentment about it can turn love into hate; on the other hand, not caring means not feeling. Thus there is considerable truth in the observation that "the opposite of love is not hate, but indifference." Regardless of a former bond and lingering feelings toward someone, it is best to carefully notice how far the other person is willing to go to get what they want.

Avoid Exhaustion and Burnout

It is exhausting to be strategic all of the time in response to conflict. No one can perpetually be on "red alert" without a risk of burning out. No matter how much you want to achieve your goals, it is important to recognize that there is no end to dealing with difficult people on your path to success and there will always be problems in one form or another. It is in your best interest to carve out some space in your life where you can put down your guard and take a break from the social game. Ideally there is at least one person in your life that you can relax with and not worry too much about strategy, conflict and power dynamics. Having a place of relative peace is most critical when dealing with antagonistic personalities. Before you have mastered your skills, your efforts will seem unnatural and require significant concentration, patience and self-control; consequently you are likely to feel like you are expending a tremendous amount of energy but getting little return. However, if you are consistent over time you will be grateful for avoiding many mistakes that others make. Eventually you will notice key opportunities that would not have otherwise presented themselves.

Transparency and Communication

Everyone has their own style of responding to conflict. Think of "style" as your very own way of approaching and responding to others. You might prefer avoidance, direct communication, retaliation, or some other style. Regardless, adapt and use the right tactic called for in any situation. While the process of actually engaging in conflict can be unpleasant, the outcome can be very positive. The best way to work out differences with others is to talk about it. Resentments and anger build up secretly, inside a person. Getting problems out in the open is critical to success in relationships and in the workplace. In the end, people who work out problems tend to have a stronger bond than those who avoid problems or simply submit to someone else. Of course conflict resolution is not always possible, but simpler methods for conflict resolution, such as direct communication, should be tried prior to using more advanced methods.

Taking Inventory

Ask yourself…

- Are you conflict-avoidant?
- Do you avoid conflict even when it is not to your

advantage?

- Do you know the difference between destructive and constructive conflict?
- What is your typical response to conflict and why?

Change Something

Do things differently...

- Stop avoiding conflict at all costs.
- Assess whether conflict is destructive or constructive.
- Prepare for the possibility of conflict long before it happens.

Develop Wisdom

Consider that...

- Conflict is sometimes inevitable and advantageous.
- Conflict can be a force for necessary change.
- There are reasons people respond to conflict differently.

Chapter 8

Law 8: What Is Given Away Freely Is Seldom Valued

Knowing others is intelligence; knowing yourself is true wisdom. Mastering others is strength; mastering yourself is true power.
—Lao Tzu, *Tao Te Ching*

It is a fact of human nature that what is easily acquired is seldom valued. If you want something to lose value, just give it away freely or make it common. Gold is not primarily valued because of its use, but because it is rare. If gold were as common as basalt rock, it would have little value. Advertisers use language like "limited offer" and artists mark their reproductions as limited, e.g. "only 100 produced," knowing that people place a higher value on something that is perceived as rare, scarce, or unavailable in the future. Research has repeatedly confirmed that rewards are valued less than identical rewards that have been earned by work or effort.

What is true with economic incentives is also true in our interactions with other people. If you give of yourself too generously, neither you nor your generosity will be appreciated. Do not make the mistake of assuming that others will like or appreciate you more because you have good intentions and a generous heart. Generosity is interpreted through the eyes of the beholder. Many people make assumptions about generosity, for example, that if something is given away, it must not have been valued very much in the first place.

If you want others to value your loyalty, respect, trust, time, energy, talents and affection, you must treat them as valuable. Imagine that your resources and positive personal qualities are like jewels of great value that you carry with you everywhere you go. Do not squander them on those who will not appreciate your generosity. Do not devalue them in the eyes of others by giving them away freely.

What Makes Us Vulnerable?

Low self-esteem, desperation, and expectations for reciprocity

There are many reasons why people give of themselves freely. Some hope that they will eventually be liked and appreciated; instead, other people sense their low self-esteem and desperation, which only makes them less attractive. Sometimes people are generous because they expect reciprocity, only to be disappointed later. Some individuals, as described in Chapter 1, project their values onto others, believing some version of the statement, "I appreciate generosity and others will appreciate it from me." Sure, sometimes people appreciate the giver of gifts and favors, but only under certain circumstances—like when the gift or favor is unexpected and without any *perception* of strings attached. But repeated acts of generosity lead others to believe that the giver has an agenda; worse, generosity becomes expected, and when stopped, resented—putting the giver in a worse position than if there had been no generosity in the first place. People are suspicious of saints, so it is not in your interest to act like one.

We give others the benefit of the doubt

We like to assume that others have at least some sense of decency until they prove us wrong. "Good people" are not supposed to look for the bad in others; everyone is supposed to be given a chance until they prove themselves wrong. Unfortunately, this chance is all the time a selfish or manipulative person needs to take advantage of generosity. We want others to appreciate us and in turn we want to appreciate others. The "takers" will keep taking while only faking appreciation.

We assume trustworthiness

Most of us try to give others the benefit of the doubt and assume that a majority of people are basically trustworthy. Even those who have been let down in the past and afterwards became cynical tend to have secret hopes about trusting others. Cynics are usually good people who have been disappointed so many times they are negative and skeptical about the motives of others. If the typical cynic actually knew that someone was trustworthy, he or she would trust again. This tendency makes them vulnerable to deceptive individuals willing to work hard to build up their trust over an extended period of time.

Make Others Earn Your Goodwill

Effort exerted increases value. The same thing gotten freely, without effort, is valued less. This response is part of human nature. "Effort" in the context of strategic engagement means requiring someone to do something before they get something from you. Even a little bit of effort makes someone appreciate something more than no effort at all. If someone asks for your help, at a minimum get them to explain the situation and why they cannot do it for themselves. Make people jump through some hoops rather than giving them easy access to what you have that is of worth. Do not impulsively run to the rescue of others unless necessary. Let people know that you too have obligations and that they should expect to wait for you to get back to them. With big requests, set conditions like, "If I help you with this big project, will you do X or Y for me?"

Making others earn your goodwill sets the stage for a productive relationship. For a relationship to be healthy, useful, or pleasurable, it must be a two-way street. Ask yourself if you are benefiting in some way when you give of yourself. If you do not take into consideration your own needs, you might find yourself in the self-defeating arrangement of giving and giving while someone else is taking and taking. There is nothing wrong with asking yourself, "What is in this for me?" After all, most people ask this question, so why not you?

Never Appear Desperate

Desperation devalues a person in the eyes of others and repels success. If you want something too badly, you will probably not get it. Frantic efforts to achieve a goal tend to drive away the very object of desire. This is analogous to what happens when someone pursues a lover too intensely—the object of love runs away. There are two reasons this happens. First, the desperate person has no choice but to wait on the mercy of the lover, therefore the lover is comfortable putting the pursuer on hold while he or she looks for something better. Second, people tend to think that someone who is desperate must not have much to offer, otherwise he or she would be accepting of rejection because they know they can find other opportunities. Just like with lovers, perceived desperation in any situation undermines your very efforts. But "perceived" is the key word. *You can desire something or someone very badly, but you must never act desperate.* Also consider that intense desire breeds errors of judgment. The desperate person commits many mistakes by being hasty and impatient, especially when lustfully drawn closer and closer to the object of desire. But none of this will be a problem for you if you recognize that you too possess something of value and that you should never put yourself in a situation where your happiness depends entirely upon something outside of your control.

Selectively Commit Your Time

People tend to think that if someone's time is valuable it will only be given out sparingly. Repeatedly giving of one's time is usually viewed as an indication of desperation, inactivity, or mediocrity. For this reason, those who are too generous with their time usually experience disrespect from others. Many people assume that "successful" people are busy and therefore not generous with their time. Another common assumption is that successful people are highly selective about who they associate with and therefore you have to work to win them over. None of these biases are facts believed by everyone, but they are pervasive enough to cause problems for generous, helpful people. Beyond these biases, repeated acts of generosity make some feel a sense of entitlement and they get angry when it stops. In order to avoid disrespect and entitlement from others, do not make yourself too available. Treat your time as precious and others will too.

Real-life experience

Dr. Moore started a primary care medical practice about a year ago. He really cared about his patients and spent extra time with them whenever he was available and needed. Sometimes he personally returned phone calls, even after hours. He was baffled when he noticed a strange pattern: many of the patients he spent the most time helping became entitled and disrespectful. He discovered that while some of his patients appreciated his efforts, others assumed that he must be desperate for patients. Some believed that he must be a second-rate physician because "successful" doctors are too busy to return calls. Certain patients even felt entitled to his time and got angry when he was too busy to go the extra mile. Dr. Moore felt hurt and angry about these experiences.

Do not make the mistake of assuming that people will appreciate it if you are generous with your time. If you freely give of your time, people are likely to assume something negative about you, regardless of whether it is due to your own passion and commitment. These guidelines even apply in romantic relationships (especially at the beginning) because withholding yourself increases the perception of your self-confidence, making you more attractive to the other person. On the other hand, when a new romantic partner is always available, the other person feels safe to stray a little bit, knowing the other person is always there, waiting for them.

The Warmest Relationships Often Start Off Cold

It might seem counter-intuitive, but when a relationship starts off rocky, but improves over time, it can become a better relationship than if there had been smooth sailing from the beginning. This is because the effort and patience exerted to make a relationship work makes someone feel like they "earned" their success. People value relationships more when they develop slowly over time. Usually the pattern early in the relationship is a version of advancing and retreating as each person tests the other over time. But do not work too hard to win someone over. As discussed in Chapter 2, some individuals cannot be won over and attempting to do so will be a waste of time and energy. If it helps, rank the people you know on a scale of 1 to 100; perhaps a 90–100 score represents a totally unwinnable person, but this is the minority.

When getting to know someone, it is *sometimes* best to intentionally—yes, intentionally!—come off as a little aloof or neutral. Let you and the other person slowly warm up to each other. This is a time of mutual evaluation. Accept some low-level negativity, like minor criticism or aloofness, as just a defensive posture that is part of the process. Neither you nor the other person should be warm and inviting. Each person should slowly and selectively accept the ideas, opinions, and interests of the other. Shared compatibilities can create a bond that is deeper than what would have been achieved from upfront "niceness." Mutual self-interest will be the key to progress in the relationship.

Real-life encounter

Laura felt negative about the new accountant, Mika, because she was jealous of her attractiveness and disliked her habit of interrupting others. Unexpectedly, the head of the firm said he was retiring. Laura and Mika found out that they were the only accountants who could afford to buy the firm. Mika invited Laura to coffee and they excitedly talked about this opportunity. Soon their mutual negativity was overshadowed by the prospect of becoming business partners. They learned that their different styles would probably be good for the business. They soon became friends.

Purge Yourself of False Assumptions about Loyalty

A common movie plot involves a deceptive villain who pretends to be on the side of the "good guys," but the deception is eventually discovered and stopped just in the nick of time, just before a catastrophic event. In the real world, however, deception can remain undiscovered until it is too late, resulting in tremendous damage without a happy ending. Prevent this from happening by replacing any false beliefs that you might have about loyalty with the following principles.

Your loyalty is worth something; therefore, it should not be given away for free

Your life is not a game where others should be given free points just because they have not acted selfishly *yet*. It is best to remember that many selfish individuals disguise themselves as wolves in sheep's clothing. Rather than getting stuck between "giving someone the benefit of the doubt" and not expecting loyalty at all, set some protective rules about loyalty. Consider the following principles.

Loyalty should not be automatically assumed

Just because someone has not been disloyal does not mean they are loyal. Have they been tested? Have they chosen to do the right thing when there was a selfish option? Have they shown a true commitment to their relationship with you? Many people should be considered neutral—neither loyal nor disloyal—until there is reason to know.

Do not be loyal to the undeserving

Those who remain loyal to the disloyal are never respected—on the contrary, they are disrespected and perceived as suckers to be taken advantage of by others. Some people will attempt to exploit a proclivity for misplaced loyalty, such as poor social judgment, an eagerness to please, or conflict-avoidance.

Do not be loyal out of guilt or penance

We have all made mistakes and at one time we too perhaps lied or hurt someone else's feelings. Many people make the mistake of remaining loyal to another person as penance for guilt, e.g. "I cheated on my wife, so I deserve to be treated like crap year after year." People in this situation find themselves trapped because the other person never lets them off the hook. Besides, guilt-motivated loyalty is rarely appreciated; for example, it would not be realistic to believe, "If I put up with mistreatment as penance for my mistake, eventually my suffering will be appreciated and I will be respected again." Having done something wrong does not justify becoming the eternal martyr.

Do not be loyal to impersonal systems

Organizations like institutions and corporations are not human beings and therefore cannot reciprocate loyalty. Your loyalty, commitment and dedication can only be reciprocated by human beings. Sure, organizations can be great employers, but those in charge still pull the strings and almost always ensure that their needs are met first—not yours. Unless you are truly in-the-know, your trust in an organization is a type of blind faith at your own risk. Many loyal employees of organizations have been strung along by stories of "dedication to our employees," only to suddenly lose their jobs. *There have even been instances of highly successful companies with record profits that shut down factories and moved operations overseas, regardless of the fact that their fantastic success was only made possible by loyal and hard-working employees.* When the people who run organizations can choose between becoming personally richer versus rewarding loyal employees, do not expect loyalty to be rewarded, regardless of success; expect loyalty to be even less of a factor when there are problems.

Violations of the Principles

Example # 1
A woman does not want to break her wedding vows so she stays with her husband even though he abuses her every day.

What is the mistake?
That a promise binds her to loyalty regardless of how her husband acts. In this case, the wife has forgotten that the purpose of the marriage vows is to increase commitment to the other person for the sake of mutual love and goodwill. Loyalty is always for a higher purpose. When that purpose disappears, so does the reason for loyalty.

Example # 2
An executive feels a sense of loyalty to his company and never looks for another job, even though his good ideas are shunned by the people above him who fear change.

What is the mistake?
Loyalty is not a one-way street. Loyalty should always be mutual. If you are loyal, but the organization is not, you are wasting your time.

Example # 3

A former friend and business partner calls up his old friend, Sheila, asking for a loan. His old friend/partner feels obligated because of their shared connection and loans him $20,000. Over time he makes up excuses why he needs more and more time to pay back the loan, ultimately creating headaches for Sheila who never gets her money back.

What is the mistake?

That the past binds someone to an obligation. Just because they were once friends and business partners is almost meaningless. Her friend probably would not have called if he did not need to borrow money.

Loyalty Should Be Strategic

In a sense, loyalty is always a little risky, but there are several principles described below to help guide you and decrease your odds of getting burned. Equally as important is learning to use the loyalty of others to your own advantage. Just like respect and trust, loyalty should not be a one-way street or even a 70/30 split. Your ability to engage others optimally may require a radical change in your way of thinking. The following are some guiding principles that will help you make loyalty work for you.

Loyalty should evolve slowly over time

Test someone incrementally to see if they are capable of being loyal. A metaphor for this is the wild mushroom: if you are lost in the woods and hungry, eating wild mushrooms could save your life, but they can also be deadly. Survivalists teach that if you are lost in the woods, hungry, and come across some wild mushrooms, you should take a small bite and wait a few minutes; if you do not get sick, then you are supposed to take a slightly larger bite, and wait a couple of hours. If you are still not sick, eat more and wait several more hours. Finally, if you do not get sick, it is probably an edible mushroom. Treat people the same way! Test the loyalty of others in little steps over time and you will decrease your odds of getting burned.

Do not be loyal at all costs

Loyalty is not supposed to be an end in itself: it serves a higher purpose. As an example, a soldier might be extremely loyal to his country, but if he has a conscience, he would never follow an order to kill an innocent child for amusement. This is because there is something higher than loyalty: your own integrity. Decide how far you are willing to go before demands are made of you.

Loyalty is not all-or-nothing

Who says that you have to either be loyal 100% or not at all, or that someone has to be 100% loyal to you? Someone might not be loyal to you all of the time, but if they can be loyal in certain situations, they can still be of use. This is especially important in specific situations. If it helps, scale your relationships from 1 to 10. Someone might not be a 10 but maybe they are a 5 on a scale of fidelity. Furthermore, someone can move from a 9 to a 4 or from any number to another, depending on their behavior.

Determine someone else's hierarchy of loyalty

Do not assume that because someone is loyal to you they are not *more loyal* to someone else. Many people get burned because they do not consider this possibility. As an example, Nick and Lorenzo might be good friends, but if Nick is angry with Lorenzo's wife, Lorenzo is likely to be more loyal to his wife and might tell her everything that Nick says. At work, do not assume that the people who sympathize with your complaints or share your ideas will stick by your side if it comes down to loyalty to you versus competing self-interests, like promotions or approval from those above them.

Self-interest can trump loyalty

When two people are loyal to each other but later find themselves competing against each other, loyalty will be tested and likely fail. Imagine three car salesmen who are also personal friends getting told, "Whoever sells the most cars this quarter gets to keep his job. The other two will get fired." Fear, insecurity, and loyalty to the families they support could outweigh their friendship and even turn them against each other. Another example is that of two or more single friends who experience sexual attraction toward the same person—their friendship will be tested. Ultimately most people are much more loyal to their own self-interests than anything else.

Introspect and Change

Examine yourself, look within, and purge yourself of any tendency to be loyal without strategizing ahead of time. Mentally adapt to the belief that no one has a right to put their happiness ahead of your own. You were not born into this world to be a punching-bag or to be taken advantage of by others. On the contrary, if you have real personal integrity and want to accomplish some good in this world, including your own version of personal success, then you are entitled to have more confidence than selfish people who only end up doing more harm than good.

Beware of Friends

Nothing—except perhaps romantic commitment—is more satisfying than friendship. But friendship is complex, not simple. Friendship is not a selfless relationship and is only possible because of mutual self-interests; once those things vanish, the friendship eventually dies. There is little chance for friendship to bloom without shared interests and pleasures. Friendship also usually requires social and economic compatibilities. Rare is the multimillionaire who is friends with the pauper; rare is the "geek" who is friends with the "jock." If levels of status or prosperity change for one friend, but not the other, the result is often jealousy and resentment. In fact, discrepancies resulting from something like getting a huge promotion while your best friend stays stuck in a lesser position usually kill a friendship. These facts are rarely, if ever, discussed or even considered. But if you are aware of such things, you will not take things so personally or painfully because you understand that some circumstances would test any friendship. *Understand and remember this unpleasant thought: a former friend or romantic partner can become an opponent, fueled by resentments from the past.* When this happens, everything they know about you can be used against you.

Avoid the Alternatives: Paranoia and Isolation

Isolation and paranoia are antithetical to success. Goodwill, trust and loyalty are necessary to have friends, collaborators, and allies. Of course relationships make us vulnerable to disappointment. Most people have at one point or another been betrayed or deceived, resulting in emotional or financial harm. Typical reactions include anger and a desire to retaliate. Those who get burned more than a few times become cynical, untrusting, and jaded. To never trust or expect loyalty is safest, but this point of view results in social isolation and the inability to accomplish anything that requires support. Very few good things in life happen without other people getting involved. For these reasons, it is crucial to know when, how, and in what measure to expect and deliver trust and loyalty.

Use the Internet

You can decrease the odds of betrayal by looking for obvious signs of untrustworthiness. Does this person have a positive track record with things such as family, education, and employment? Does this person have a criminal history? Do not fear "snooping" on someone by looking into records with the aid of an internet background search company such as Intelius; Instant Checkmate; US Search; BeenVerified; PeopleWise; PeopleSmart; PeopleFinders; Verispy; Inteligator, or BackgroundReport.com. These internet search companies charge for their services, but knowing who you are dealing with in important relationships is vitally important for your safety and welfare. Sometimes these background searches can be wrong and should not be automatically accepted as fact, but what facts you do have might confirm or disconfirm the report.

Do Not Give Away Your Privacy or Confidentiality

Regardless of the trust and loyalty of others, it is critical to *never* assume complete privacy or confidentiality. Many people have been burned by confiding in someone who appeared trustworthy but later told others what was said in secret. Many "confidential" sources of health information and anonymous websites have been leaked or hacked. Due to social media, billions of individuals are more publicly accessible than ever before. It might be better to put more effort into shaping a positive image than into avoiding the limelight. Be careful with digital words and images that can be used against you permanently.

Taking Inventory

Ask yourself…

- Has your generosity gone unreciprocated?
- Have you been trustworthy and loyal, only to get burned?
- Despite generosity with your time, affection, or talents, do others not respect you or do they act entitled to what you share?

Change Something

Do things differently...

- Make others earn what you have before you share anything.
- Be prudent and let loyalty evolve slowly over time.
- Selectively give of your time.

Develop Wisdom

Consider that...

- What you have is worth something. Act like it.
- By nature, humans do not value what is common or easily acquired.
- Relationships matter—no man is an island.

Chapter 9

Law 9: Treat Others According to the Role They Play

Democracy arose from men's thinking that if they are equal in any respect they are equal absolutely in all respects.
— Aristotle

Successful social engagement requires changing tactics based upon your position in relationship to someone else. Just as it would be unwise for a small army to use the same tactics as a large army, any disadvantage you have compared to others requires an adjustment in tactics. Begin by comparing the level of power, authority, and influence you or your group has in relation to others. If you possess fewer critical resources, such as numerical support or power, use minority tactics to turn disadvantage into advantage. Consider some of the following roles each of us has in relation to others:

Advantaged	Disadvantaged
Majority	Minority
Familiar	Unfamiliar
High Power	Low Power
High Resource	Low Resource
Expert	Non-Expert

While most of us understand the difference between roles like "father" and "husband," or "employee" and "employer," few think about bigger categories that they fall into wherever they go. The following spells out some specific tactics that can be used to win regardless of a disadvantaged role.

Minority Tactics

If you find yourself in a minority role begin by deciding whether or not your primary goal is to *influence* or *persuade* the majority. Winning someone totally to your side might be desirable, but it is not always realistic. It is much easier to influence others than to change their minds. The more contrarian to conventional ideas, the more resistance you will face. People do not like to make sacrifices or have their opinions challenged. But remember that all majorities were once minorities and that the marketing of good ideas with wide appeal can change hearts and minds.

To be effective, a minority must *appear credible, use sound arguments, stay consistent, and be willing to compromise.* Missing any of these four approaches can result in failure. Deceptive tactics—if discovered—will taint the messenger and the message. Avoid seeming morally superior, preachy, or scolding; do not demand sacrifices or be unwilling to negotiate. Be firm and moderately repetitive about the main issue. Be patient and plan for the long term. Do not assume that being "right" all by itself will sell an idea for you—it is usually not enough.

Above all, appeal to the self-interest of the majority. This can be done in one of two ways: positively (how things will get better if there is change) and negatively (how something undesirable will go away if there is change). Let others know how they will benefit from adopting the minority position and how not changing will result in problems. It is less than ideal, but sometimes expected, that the majority simply gets worn down enough to compromise in order to cease conflict and stop the drain of time and attention required to respond to a vocal minority.

Use First Impressions to Your Advantage

First impressions can have a long-lasting, deep impact upon the minds of others. Psychologists call this phenomenon the *primacy effect*. What someone experiences when meeting a new person or learning about a new group tends to mentally "stick" with them. This might not seem fair, but at least you can anticipate it and respond optimally. *There are three primary ways to make a positive first impression: the use of charm, rapport building, and building expectations.* During first encounters, more important things like personal character or the merit of an idea are usually less important than first impressions.

Charm has to do with things such as self-confidence and likeability. People who come across as secure and well-balanced have universal appeal. At a minimum, people want to know if an unfamiliar person is safe, "normal," friendly and inviting. This helps them decide whether you make them comfortable enough to accept your pitch for change, even if they might disagree. Do not neglect details like appropriate physical appearance or style. New ideas can be scary enough, but an eccentric or unusual presentation will be unnecessary distractions that compound fear of change. *Rapport building* involves showing an interest in others in a non-judgmental way. Listening, providing positive feedback (including a timely sense of humor), and conveying that you like someone are core elements of rapport building. *Building expectations* involves exuding confidence and conveying that you can meet or beat expectations. Even if you have some self-doubts, pump up expectations anyhow because once people believe you, they tend to become invested in their own assumptions. People with invested expectations are more likely to notice your positives and less likely to take a negative attitude from the beginning.

Low Resource & Power Tactics

To have less time, money, or power is a huge disadvantage. Options will be limited. However, there is such a thing as "soft power," which is an indirect type of influence using such means as *values affinity, seduction, and personality.* Someone who shares your religion, culture, or political point of view might favor you regardless of your power or resources. Seduction involves appealing to base appetites like sexual interest or some kind of indulgent, decadent temptation. A seductive appeal works best when it is present, but not overtly emphasized. A winning personality that is entertaining, charismatic, or lifts the spirits of others can have great appeal.

Non-Expert Tactics

Have you ever noticed that specialists and technical experts only sometimes get to the very top of organizations? Unlike Bill Gates and Steve Jobs, many CEOs of technology companies do not even have a background in product innovation or development. This is also true of low-technology companies. This is because good leadership does not require extensive technical knowledge. For example, developers with good ideas do not need to be architects or builders to build skyscrapers; they use others to do these things for them. Consider that a military leader in wartime does not need to understand everything about how a tank or ship was engineered in order to be effective. *Similarly, a leader with good judgment who is able to see the big picture knows how to use people with specialized skills, but the reverse is not necessarily true: those with specialized skills do not always see the big picture or have good judgment.* It follows that if you are a non-expert you should not bother to argue with experts on their turf where you will lose — instead, focus upon macro topics like how decisions impact people, priorities, values, organization, and the overall grand vision for success.

Avoid Totally Leveling the Playing Field

In many parts of the world, especially in the West, people believe in democratic values. We tend to believe that everyone has rights, individual worth, and that laws should apply to everyone, regardless of wealth or class. These ideas are sometimes reinforced by religions that teach that God values the life of every human being. These kinds of beliefs—right or wrong—lead some individuals to conclude that everyone should be treated basically the same whenever possible. This is a mistake that can result in unnecessary conflicts and unintended consequences.

Human attitudes and perceptions of others are highly based on where they stand in relation to others' positions of power or authority. *Individuals high in power or authority will have great difficulty getting others to see past their social roles; those in lower positions cannot exceed their roles without punishment from those above them.* The following suggestions provide protection against errors associated with role confusion:

Avoid assuming that others can see past your role

Most people will respect a leader who makes good decisions that benefit everyone. This should be satisfaction enough for someone in a leadership position. Expect more and you set yourself up for problems. Do not expect to be liked and respected for your humanity over your social role.

> *Example of the false assumption: "I might be in charge of the organization, but I want people to see me as being just like them"*
>
> *A CEO of a mid-sized company feels like he is "just a regular guy" and demonstrated his concern and commitment to employees by showing up for low-level meetings and "hanging out" with regular employees at community events. At first some of the employees were suspicious of him, but over time most got used to his presence. Some*

got casual, using profanity in his presence. Eventually he started hearing things like, "Aren't you rich? Must be nice," and "Let me tell you what really sucks about this company," and "Why don't you give me a raise?" Not everyone said these things; most employees treated him well. Others shied away from him, suspicious about his intentions. Eventually the CEO became so uncomfortable with these interactions that he abruptly stopped hanging out with his employees.

The mistake the CEO made was that he expected his employees to see beyond his role as a CEO and not be distracted by his authority over them and greater financial compensation. The CEO's well-intentioned attempt was doomed to fail because no matter how familiar a leader becomes, the primary role will overshadow others' roles. There are of course exceptions; for example, sometimes a successful leader who worked his way to success will relate to others who appreciate his humble background. But social roles demarcate relationships and cannot usually be minimized, even between teachers and students, priests and parishioners, and supervisors and employees. Familiarity can mitigate the distance created by some social roles. A first-line supervisor of a small to medium-sized business will have more success identifying and socializing with employees than the vice-president of a large company. A priest will find it easier to relate to parishioners than a cardinal. A mayor might connect with constituents in a more personal and casual way than a senator. Trying to relate with others too far removed from your role is always risky and should be done with caution. Perhaps your equals or family members can see past your role, but not necessarily others.

Familiarity can lead to role confusion

What about in work-related situations where someone in a low-power position becomes too familiar with someone in a higher position? This is risky and can create a false sense of comfort and importance that is eventually resented. Consider the following scenario.

Example of employee and employer role confusion

A receptionist has worked closely with her employer, a small business owner, for about three years. The business owner treats her with respect, asks her opinion on business matters, and from time to time they even spend free time together, meeting for coffee or shopping. The receptionist has become so familiar and social with the owner that she begins treating her like an equal. She has taken certain liberties like making more decisions without asking and once in a while telling her what decisions to make. The business owner has become secretly resentful that she has been taking these liberties, but feels stuck because she helped create this dynamic. Sometimes she just wants to give blunt instructions without conversation or emotions, but doing so makes her uncomfortable because she feels like a friend. One day she blows up at the receptionist for making a mistake and fires her. The receptionist was in tears and felt betrayed, baffled, and extremely resentful.

In the above situation, both parties are at fault. Clearly the owner had poor boundaries and could have dealt with her discomfort before it became a crisis. But the receptionist—being in a position of low power—had more to lose. Familiarity led to role confusion and she felt as if her role as an employee was supplanted by friendship with the owner. In the end she lost her job, but her expectations for friendship doubled her emotional pain.

Put a check on emotions

Accepting one's role (outside of personal relationships) requires emotional detachment. Sometimes people need to be told "No," or "You're fired," and will only resent it more if you try to soften the blow.

Example of impractical emotional attachment

Kelli was the supervisor of a small department and had a problem employee, Linda, who could not cope with the stress of the job and was slow and inefficient. Unfortunately, she had to be terminated. Kelli knew Linda on a personal level and that she was a kind and sensitive person, and sadly her family needed her income, but she was totally incapable of doing the job correctly. Kelli called Linda into her office and apologetically told Linda that she was getting fired and explained how sad she felt about it. Kelli said it "wasn't personal," that Linda would be missed, and that she hoped things would work out for her in the future.

Linda did not appreciate Kelli's apology and thought that Kelli must be doing something wrong to feel so badly about her termination. Kelli was surprised and shocked to learn that Linda complained to human resources about Kelli and said that her behavior was unprofessional. Linda was even considering filing a lawsuit. Kelli was completely bewildered. She had been so patient with Linda, so kind, and expressed so much goodwill, and had conveyed how hard and painful it was to let her go! How could Linda do this?

Regardless of how badly you feel about having to do something unpleasant, when it comes to anything painful your actions will always carry more weight than your sweet or mournful sentiments. When someone is angry about your decision, they will perceive your good nature as a weakness to exploit. They might even resent you more for self-righteously trying to soothe your conscience in their time of difficulty. Instead of being timid and apologetic, be bold when you have to make tough decisions. You will be more respected for your assertiveness than you will ever be appreciated for how badly you felt when you caused someone else pain.

Role confusion in families

The above principles apply in personal relationships as well. Think of each person within a family or a personal relationship as having separate roles with different responsibilities. When these lines get blurred, there is confusion. Many dysfunctional families experience role confusion; similarly, many healthy families have some dysfunction due to the same issue. Consider the following three examples of role confusion within families.

Example # 1 of familial role confusion

A father knows that his teenage daughter loves him, but he also wants her to like him all of the time. To accomplish this, he goes to great lengths to make sure she is never upset or angry with him. He treats her more like a friend than a daughter. He avoids using his parental authority in any way that makes her unhappy so that she will always approve of him. As expected, his daughter increasingly pushes limits and gets away with a lot of risky behavior, like staying out late and spending too much money. Eventually the father cannot take it anymore and confronts her, but by then it is too late. She reacts with rage. He backs down because he is afraid she might not like him anymore if he persists.

Example # 2 of familial role confusion

Jane is a single mom without any friends. She has a lot of problems and talks to her son about all of her problems, just like he was an adult friend. Her son has his own problems and can hardly cope, but he loves his mom so he keeps acting like her friend, but sometimes it feels like he is her therapist.

Example # 3 of familial role confusion

Everyone tells Cindy that her daughter, Stephanie, is taking advantage of her. Stephanie is 29 years old but is unemployed, does not look for work, lives at home, and never helps out around the house. She treats her mom with disrespect. Cindy has always been a "care-giver" type person and "needs to be needed." Cindy knows it is not healthy for Stephanie to be dependent upon her, but she can't bear the thought of living alone.

The above three examples are characterized by an emotional dependency that is highly unhealthy for each parent. Each child is also in an unhealthy situation as the parents reinforce poor boundaries, irresponsibility, and dependency. Remember the saying "The way to hell is paved with good intentions"? It is well-intentioned to want to be loved, needed, liked, and to get support by talking about one's problems. But when family roles are confused and parents do not act like parents, these good intentions actually harm their own children who do not learn independence or who feel emotionally burdened by their parents.

In Summary

Those of high power/authority should not confuse others by becoming too familiar and overly accessible. Those in lower power/authority positions should not over-reach their authority, no matter how inviting the temptation. Avoid imposing democratic values in inappropriate situations. It does *not* follow that because every human being has worth, therefore, everyone's opinion should be solicited or that everyone should be treated the same. Even in personal relationships roles matter and ignoring them results in dysfunctional dynamics.

Taking Inventory

Ask yourself…

- What are your unspoken roles in social situations?
- Do you know what it takes to win, despite having a disadvantageous role?

Change Something

Do things differently...

- Appeal to the majority using successful minority tactics.
- Make a positive first impression with charm, rapport, and expectations.
- Use soft power to your advantage.
- Do not expect others to see beyond your social role.

Develop Wisdom

Consider that...

- A leader is someone with good judgment who sees the big picture—not necessarily someone with highly specialized skills.
- Democratic values do not level the playing field of life 100 percent.
- Respect yourself and others by honoring whatever roles you possess.

Chapter 10

Law 10: Never Take on Another Person's Burden as If It Was Your Own

There has never been a man who could straighten others by bending himself.
—Confucius

While your resources are finite, the neediness of others is nearly infinite. Even a billionaire would quickly become impoverished if he or she thoughtlessly wrote out checks to every needy person. Thus you must think strategically and make an effort to develop boundaries and limits to the extent of your generosity. Avoiding extremes is necessary. Stinginess is foolish because your resources should serve you on your path to success, not be hoarded. On the other hand, excessive generosity will deprive you of essential resources needed for your efforts. The two aspects to consider are proportion and image. How much and when should you help others with time, money, or personal favors? Beyond that, your reputation is built upon the image you convey, therefore it is crucial that you avoid appearing selfish or uncaring (hopefully, because you really are unselfish and caring!). If others perceive you as unhelpful or greedy, they will at the very least become unsupportive, but even worse, they might learn to despise you. The following principles can serve as a guide to help you maximize the good that you do for yourself and others, regardless of whether you have few or many resources at your disposal.

Act Philanthropically from Surplus, Not Deficit

It is true but paradoxical that helping yourself allows you to help others. If you are too generous and leave nothing for yourself, you will have nothing left to give. To use an analogy, there is a reason why flight attendants instruct passengers that in the event of an emergency they should put on their own oxygen masks before attending to others—even their own children. You are no good to anyone else if you are unconscious. Just as with oxygen masks on a plane, assisting others should be a matter of sharing your resources after you have approached a comfortable point of safety. People who think they should go out of their way to make huge sacrifices to others usually end up spending themselves out of the very resources needed to continue their sacrifices. Make sure that when you give to others it is out of your own surplus, not deficit.

Match Your Generosity to Self-Interest

A long time ago the ancient Roman statesman Cicero wrote about how the wise person will always look for an advantage when trying to do "the right thing." His point was that there are times in life when helping another person also benefits you. But rather than hoping for a happy coincidence, you should form a strategic intention to benefit from every action you undertake. Rather than indiscriminately helping others, ask yourself whether you can "kill two birds with one stone" by simultaneously attaining some benefit in the process, e.g. "David did not want to help Kesha, but then he remembered that she controlled the travel budget and he wanted to attend a seminar in another state." While finding an advantage in helping someone is not always possible, the more conscious you are of this intention, the more opportunities you will perceive. Even small amounts of generosity can be helpful; for example, buying lunch for a possible future client may pay great dividends in the future. It is not selfish to look for ways to benefit when helping others unless you *only* help others when it is to your benefit. Remember from Chapter 1 that self-interest is not the same as selfishness.

Recognize That Needy People Usually Do Not Disclose All Their Resources

It only makes sense that someone will begin asking others for favors *before* they experience a crisis. Fear compels us to seek help before we have exhausted all of our own resources. As an example, if I only have $50 but owe someone else $100, I would rather borrow $100 from you to pay back the other person so that I could keep $50 for myself and avoid destitution. Versions of this kind of resource protection occur all the time in different settings, including among rich people and corporations. Smart people borrow cheap to pay down debt, if possible, rather than use their own resources. If you doubt the truth of this proposition, test someone. The next time you withhold a favor of some kind, see whether or not the other person finds a way to survive or adapt to the problem. Usually, they find a way! The point of this observation is not to discourage you from being generous; rather, it is to help you avoid becoming overly burdened by someone else's problems. Most of the time if you do not help someone, they will survive; in fact, they have probably already survived so many years on this planet without your help. Except in very special and rare cases, no one's entire life or happiness depends upon a single act of your generosity.

"Help Me" Can Be Manipulation in Disguise

Another reason to be careful when someone asks for help is that it can be a manipulation tactic. If someone seems to need help or is vulnerable in some way, do not immediately jump to save them. Get information first. Is there some evidence this person really cannot help his or her self? Is this person trying to the best of his or her ability to help themselves? Is there a pattern of burnout among others who have tried to help? Does the person asking for help have a tendency to repeatedly cause their own problems? Does generosity enable dysfunctional dependency or encourage feelings of entitlement? Most of us feel good when we help others. We feel honored that someone would trust us enough to help them. However, in order to avoid getting taken advantage of by others we must use good judgment in deciding when and how to help others. There is nothing wrong with being cautious; after all, the most typical tactic of a conman is to lure others into a situation by appearing fragile or needy.

When Helping Others, Expect Little in Return

Other people are not selfless angels looking forward to doing favors for you. When you expect reciprocity, you give away your power by letting someone else decide whether they will return the favor while you patiently wait at their mercy. Instead, focus upon what is within your control when you do favors for others, and expect little or nothing in return. If some favor is requited, you will get a pleasant surprise; if not, you will not feel crushed and defeated.

Consider the following two versions of the same scenario. In the first scenario Jill has hopes that lead to disappointment; in the second scenario she realistically focuses on things within her control.

Scenario A (expectations lead to disappointment)

Jill was a lead reporter for a local newspaper. She went out of her way to make sure that the new reporter, Mike, had all the help he needed to be successful in his new job. She believed that if Mike ever put his administrative skills to use at the company, he would remember all her help. She was baffled when he got promoted and seemed to forget all about her. Mike even supported budget cuts that might have eliminated her job.

Scenario B (better response with realistic expectations)

Jill was a lead reporter for a local newspaper. She went out of her way to make sure that the new reporter, Mike, had all the help he needed to be successful in his new job. She decided to do this because so many others had helped her along the way in her career. She was careful not to expect anything in return, and realized that Mike's character hadn't been tested—maybe he would be grateful; maybe he would throw her under the bus if the temptation was right. When he got promoted he seemed to forget all about her. Jill still felt good about what she did because she didn't do it just for Mike, but for herself. Her expectations were realistic.

Having realistic expectations about others requires us to detach from outcomes we cannot control. We control our intentions and actions, but not those of others, including whether someone will appreciate our generosity, kindness, or favors.

Here is another identical situation but with two different responses:

Scenario A (expectations lead to disappointment)

Cory gave $30 to a homeless woman expecting her to use it for basic needs. He was angry after he saw her go into a liquor store.

Scenario B (better response with realistic expectations)

Cory gave $30 to a homeless woman as an act of charity. But before he even gave her the money he reminded himself that he had no control over how she spent the money: she could use it to help herself; on the other hand, she could buy any number of things with it—food, clothing, liquor, or a knife to kill someone—anything she could afford. But he detached from worrying about the outcome by reminding himself that whatever she did was outside of his control. A few minutes later he saw her go into a liquor store, but he did not get angry. He thought to himself, "While it was my goal to be chari-table, it was her responsibility to spend it right. I did my part; she did not do hers, but I am not responsible for her actions." He even felt good about what he did because he did what was right, which is all he was responsible for doing.

If you paused to critique the practice of giving money directly to the homeless, you are missing the point. Even large non-profits with good track records can turn out to be corrupt, but that is also outside of your control and does not diminish the fact that by giving money you did what you thought was right. Help for the sake of helping, not for the guarantee of a return on your investment or a tax write-off. (One way to check if your donation is being spent wisely is to visit a website such as http://www.charitynavigator.org where they track the actual spending of the donations received and rate non-profits' financial responsibility.)

Know How to Give and Receive Favors

When you expect reciprocity, you give away your power by letting someone else decide whether they will return the favor while you patiently wait at their mercy. But even if you avoid this error, those around you will continue to expect reciprocity, even when you do not! Therefore, you must know the right approach to giving and receiving favors. Focus upon what is within your control when you do favors for others, expecting little or nothing in return. If a favor is returned to you it will be a pleasant surprise; if not, you are safer for having taken precautions ahead of time.

Which of the following two requests is most likely to motivate someone to help you?

"I am stressed out and overworked. Will you cover for me so I can take a couple of days off?"
"I would like to take a couple of days off. If you cover for me, I will work a couple of days for you whenever you want it."

Obviously the second sentence is much more compelling because it appeals to someone's self-interest. Voicing a complaint and hoping for someone to volunteer assistance is much less effective than appealing to someone's needs or desires. Whenever possible, offer others favors in return rather than expecting "free" help.

Should you expect others to return favors? If you helped someone out in the past, will they be willing to help you in your time of need? The answer is, "it depends on what kind of person you are dealing with." The "takers" of the world will not repay you, will repay very little, or will expect bigger favors from you than you did for them.

Dispense Favors Intermittently, But Give Bad News All at Once

It is best to bestow favors in small increments, intermittently, rather than all at once. Favors given all at once are temporarily uplifting, but eventually people return to their baseline level of happiness and again begin hoping for more. Too much liberality can result in a person "topping out" as the giver becomes unable to match any previous level of generosity, while others continue to expect the pattern of increasing generosity. Moreover, when generosity is very great, even when deserved for outstanding work, the recipients might begin to believe they are better than others and view as inconsequential the very favors they were granted. When favors are bestowed unpredictably, the anticipation others experience will make them appreciate more the good you are attempting to accomplish. It is even better to do this on a schedule of what psychologists call a *variable ratio*. This is an intermittent, unpredictable means of granting rewards. Here are two examples of "bad" and "better" approaches to dispensing rewards:

Bad method and response:

Five of the top performers at a brokerage firm got huge annual bonuses for the third year in a row. They were so emboldened by their success that they became arrogant, looked down on their superiors, and eventually began searching for top executive positions at other companies.

Better method and response:

Five of the top performers at a brokerage firm received quarterly bonuses in unpredictable amounts, not all at once. They kept their arrogance in check because they did not know the formula for bonuses nor did they want to irk management and jeopardize the possibility of a bonus next quarter.

Bad method and response:

A housekeeper only makes minimum wage, but was tipped $15 every time for two hours of work. This increased her salary by one-third. At first she was grateful, but later came to expect it and resented anything less than $15.

Better method and response:

A housekeeper is tipped anywhere from $4 to $15 for her work. She never knew how much the tip would be, so she did good work without feeling entitled to a specific amount of tip.

Virtually every one of us, if given a choice, would prefer to have the things we desire "right now" rather than letting someone else dole them out over time. But the research makes it clear that what people appreciate most is not what they say they want, but intermittent positive experiences. Retail stores know all about this and alternate "regular" with "sale" prices. When the retail store J.C. Penney decided to market the idea that there would be no more sales because every product was "on sale" all of the time, sales quickly plummeted and the idea was scrapped. Slot machines also provide a good model for reinforcement; they are addictive because they pay out unpredictably. Make sure your favors are appreciated by including these aspects of human nature in the equation.

On the other hand, in order to avoid resentment from others, it is better to give bad news all at once, not little by little. It will not ease someone's pain if they are informed in a piecemeal way about something negative. Instead, they will become more suspicious about whether you are withholding information. They will resent uncertainty as they speculate about more bad news to come. If you are in a position of power, others will use their spare time to plead and negotiate with you to change your mind, even when this is not possible or practical. If someone is against you, they will use their time to undermine you and your efforts. Pull the band-aid off; do not tug slowly. As an economic corollary, studies have shown that people have less resentment when prices are raised all at once, and remain stable, rather than when prices increase little by little over time.

Do Not Be the Accountant in Close Relationships

Close, personal relationships should be characterized by reciprocity, but avoid thinking like an accountant calculating a balance sheet. Friends and lovers cannot be treated economically. It would not make sense, for example, for a husband to write down every little thing his wife does for him so he could even the ledger by doing things for her. The closer you are to someone, the more you do things spontaneously, from the "goodness of your heart," as the saying goes. But this can be dangerous as well. When you are not keeping track of favors, instances of disrespect, lack of affection and the absence of reciprocity can suddenly hit you in the face. It is a terrible experience when you suddenly realize a pattern of being taken advantage of and that your friend or committed partner is a taker while you are the giver. Keep track of reciprocity, but do not become obsessive about it in order to avoid getting taken advantage of by others.

Taking Inventory

Ask yourself...

- Have you been generous, maybe too generous, and others do not appreciate it?
- Have you been stingy to the point where others do not believe you are generous at all?
- Do you know how to give and receive favors in an optimal way?

Change Something

Change something about yourself...

- Understand that it is not selfish to find ways to help oneself while also helping others.
- Set limits to giving and avoid the extremes of stinginess and excessive generosity.
- Always consider *how* to be generous rather than simply expecting to be appreciated.
- Do not make rewards excessive or predictable if you want people to appreciate them.

Develop Wisdom

Consider that...

- The needs and wants of some people are never-ending.
- It is possible to have genuine concern for others and yet detach from their suffering.
- Even when they say otherwise, people are more willing to help when they think they might get something in return.

Chapter 11

Law 11: The Majority Prefer Fantasy Over Harsh Realities

Lying to ourselves is more deeply ingrained than lying to others.
—Fyodor Dostoevsky

Think of accepting "reality" as a hard thing, not an easy thing. Of course everyone says they want to know the "truth" and the "facts," but in actuality people go to great lengths to avoid painful realities. To consciously accept a painful or harsh reality is a hard thing—whether it is something we as individuals cannot control, like starvation and wars, or more benign, like when your favorite sports team really is the worst team. Naturally, most people dislike thinking about their problems longer than necessary. Life is full of distractions to help us avoid thinking about our own suffering, painful memories, and unsolvable problems. Our subconscious mind has a host of defense mechanisms that provide an alternative to reality and protect us from suffering.

In this chapter, "fantasy" means believing alternatives to facts—not because they *are* true but because we *want* to believe they are true. This is rarely a conscious experience. No one wakes up one morning and thinks, "Today I will believe something false because I want to feel good." Instead, it happens automatically because we are biologically hard-wired to be averse to any form of pain, including psychological pain. The greater the assault on our psyches, the more our defenses come to the rescue.

Examples of Fantasies

The following include some perhaps overly simplistic examples to help you get the "gist" of certain kinds of fantastical thinking. If you pay attention to what people say and their reasoning, you will notice they are quite common.

- **The cult of personality:** "This politician will solve all of our problems."
- **Simplistic thinking:** "If people would just be nice, we could all get along."
- **Assuming that others will prefer a painful truth over a pleasant fiction:** "People would rather know the truth over what they want to hear."
- **The illusion of total objectivity:** "My judgments and perceptions are never biased."
- **Ignoring the possibility of a hidden motive:** "People say he compliments me because he wants something from me, but I know he means it."
- **An ego blinded to seduction:** "People tell me she just wants my money, but I know true love when I see it."
- **Generalizing character from vague and untested observations:** "She's always professional and friendly, so I know I can trust her."

The Self-Misperception Fantasy

What most people think of themselves tends to be a little too glowing. Research indicates that most people think they are smarter, better-looking, and more liked than they are in real life. Most people describe themselves as self-confident and optimistic. Research has shown that 70–90% of people judge themselves to be "above average" in major life areas like marriage, occupation, happiness, and physical appearance, but by definition this is not possible. "Above average" is by definition less than "the majority," which would be "average." Ironically, sometimes people who are slightly depressed actually perceive reality a little more clearly because they are not over-confident or unrealistically optimistic. Not surprisingly, those who suffer from more severe depression have the opposite problem from most of us: they are prone to extremes of exaggerating negativity and self-blame. Reality is usually somewhere in-between an inflated self-image and self-deprecation.

The self-serving bias

Another example of self-misperception is what psychologists call the *self-serving bias*. Most people have a tendency to take credit for successes while externalizing blame for failures, e.g. "I deserved that promotion, but it was unfair when they laid me off." "She liked me because I'm a catch. She left me because she's stupid." The upside of the self-serving bias is that it protects our ego; the downside is that blaming others prevents us from taking responsibility for our actions, which is required for self-improvement. Accepting reality sometimes means that we should not take credit for every success nor should we blame others for every failure. Overcome the self-serving fantasy by trying to be objective. If you are not responsible for something bad, great, but if you played a role in it, learn from the experience without becoming overly self-critical. Accept that many circumstances in life result from subtle combinations of choices and external forces.

What is the reason that human beings have a proclivity toward inflated sense of self? One theory is that it gave us an evolutionary edge. In times past, inaction from despair and low motivation would have resulted in fewer food-seeking behaviors and therefore death. This is the background that the human psyche evolved from, so it is not surprising that most of us naturally seek out the positives in life, no matter how dark things appear. Optimism can give us confidence and help us make good decisions in life. It can also be a false path that keeps us from quitting something when we would be wise to put our energy elsewhere. But it is not necessary to wear rose-colored glasses. Is the proverbial glass half-empty or half-full? In reality the glass is simultaneously both half empty and full. This is a realist's perspective and the ideal perspective for engaging social reality.

The halo effect bias

Several studies have proven that when people identify one desirable trait in someone, such as intelligence, athletic ability, or attractiveness, they tend to assume that person also has other desirable personality traits, such as trustworthiness, leadership ability, and self-discipline. This is called the *halo effect* and it is, of course, irrational. The halo effect occurs on a subconscious level. Few people would admit to judging someone simply due to a superficial trait, but in fact, it is the norm. Physical attractiveness, for example, tells us nothing about legal culpability, but studies have shown that physically attractive litigants in court tend to have more favorable outcomes than less attractive individuals. Attractive political candidates have better odds of getting elected. People unconsciously associate attractiveness with other positive traits. But this phenomenon is associated with other characteristics, such as intelligence and desirable personality traits. A similar bias also occurs when we notice something very specifically positive about someone and then generalize it to other areas about that person. If a chef is known for making an exquisite dish, people are likely to assume— without evidence—that he or she also makes other excellent dishes. This kind of assumption can result in all kinds of problems in the workplace and within personal relationships. Many businesses have promoted individuals that were highly successful in one field only to find out later they did not excel in other fields. Romantic relationships have failed after one partner learns they were seduced by a few desirable traits in another person, only to later discover many intolerable character flaws.

The in-group bias

There are many other kinds of biases that influence us to have an unjustified, favorable view of others. Having something in common with someone else is enough to have an advantage. This tends to be true even when differences are trivial. Someone of similar age, background, and life experiences is likely to be given preferential treatment over those who are different. This is also true for groups. The group someone belongs to—sometimes called the in-group—is likely to be viewed by members as superior to other groups. Members will treat each other better than outsiders. Those who no longer fit in to a group find themselves at risk of getting punished by that group.

Cognitive dissonance

The human mind is sometimes like a paradox: able to simultaneously hold sincere beliefs but act in a way contrary to those beliefs without even recognizing the contradiction. The term for this is "cognitive dissonance." The cause is the unpleasant inner conflict we feel when our morals and ethics run into conflict with antithetical desires or short-term goals. How does someone reconcile "Smoking is wrong, but I smoke"? Some people who smoke even criticize others who smoke! But this is an easy example; there are countless variations. For example, consider any good quality we believe we "should" possess. Just about everyone believes in being fair, generous, kind, loving, thoughtful, etc. but few really even make it an entire week in their lives living up to their own values 100 percent. Have you ever met someone who claimed to be fair but was preferential toward a particular person? Even when confronted with obvious contradictions, most individuals try to justify or rationalize their behavior. Cognitive dissonance is a universal human phenomenon.

Consider the fact that most chronically selfish people believe that they are fundamentally good people. This is a contradiction that is protected by the defense of denial or externalization of blame, e.g. "I lied, but you put me in a position where I had to lie!" "I am going to look out only for myself, but I am still a good person." Of course, selfish or not, every one of us has some kind of dilemma like this from time to time. Each of us tends to see ourselves as moral, compassionate, forgiving, disciplined, and having a lot of virtues, whether or not we truly live according to such qualities. People tend to experience feelings of guilt and shame when they do not live up to their own standards; in response, our minds try to protect us from negative ruminations that could sap our motivation.

The ambiguity bias

The world is filled with so much information, choices, and stimulation—in fact, more than ever in human history by a long-shot—that it is necessary to take mental shortcuts in order to be efficient. For most of us, pondering something deeply is a luxury. These shortcuts, or "mental hacks," save us time, but make us vulnerable to mistakes. One mental shortcut is a preference for what is familiar, even if it is not ideal, rather than taking a risk on an unknown. This is called the *ambiguity effect*. For example, if there were only two doctors in a small town, one with mixed rankings and a second, new and without ranking, most people would choose the doctor with average rankings rather than take a risk on an unknown doctor. Someone is more likely to purchase a car with a known history, even if it is mediocre, rather than an equivalent car with no known history. We fear that the unknown could be worse than the known, but this is not always rational and can result in missed opportunities.

The anchoring bias

One mental hack people tend to use is placing too much value on what is learned *first* about something. Think of it like having a bias in favor of a starting point. Sometimes this bias comes from our early family experiences; for example, if a person was raised in a family where watching television six hours a day was "normal," that person is likely to be surprised if they are criticized for "only" watching television three hours a day. Another example: catching a new social contact in a lie might bias others against that person for years to come, despite the fact that he or she rarely lies and is ordinarily just as honest as most people. This phenomenon is called the *anchoring bias* and can result in false assumptions about behavior.

The attentional bias

The concept of *attentional bias* essentially allows us to understand better the people we know. The things individuals value most are the lenses through which they interpret their experiences. The extreme example for this is set by the drug addict for whom everything—family, money, career, relationships—is viewed from the perspective of "how can these things help or hinder me in getting more drugs?" Just like the drug addict, there are often one or two things that someone prizes above other things. Do you want to know what someone thinks about? It is not necessarily difficult. Simply find out what someone focuses their attention upon. Is someone meticulous about something like appearance or hygiene? Then that is what they think about—perhaps not all of the time, but regularly. Is someone complaining about problems at work, physical pain, or praising their children—then these are the things that person thinks about. Sure, there are no few things that someone *only* thinks about, but consider that *the mind is like a magnifying glass: whatever we focus upon gets bigger*. Naturally people devote attention to key areas that are most important to them—whether it involves loved ones, like the welfare of one's children, or harmful subjects, like preoccupations with food, alcohol, painful memories, or fear of criticism. When the center of orbit is this or that particular thing, people are at risk of interpreting everything else in that context. Just as planets revolve around the sun, the parts of a person's life often revolve around what they value and think about most.

Increase Reality-Based Thinking

Put a check on your biases by becoming aware of them. Our minds automatically try to protect us from painful realities by deceiving us in various ways. But like a mirage that appears real, once you figure out that it is an illusion, you are no longer deceived, but free to go in the right direction. This is not merely an intellectual decision to know the "truth"; it must be practiced to become habitual. Start by identifying how cognitive fantasies influence your beliefs and behaviors.

Examples of common biases:

- Giving the advantage to someone over another because they did you a favor or have some things in common with you
- Believing that when your favorite team loses, it's due to bad luck or cheating, not because they are an inferior team
- After the fact saying, "I knew it all along"
- Getting overly impressed by superficial traits such as beauty or personality
- When things go well, crediting ourselves; when things go poorly, externalizing blame
- Overcompensating: if you can't get something you want, you despise it
- Refusing to accept the likelihood of bad news
- Preferring media that confirms one particular world-view
- Rationalizing bad behavior with excuses, e.g. "He deserved it!"

What is the antidote to biases? First of all, be brutally honest with yourself. Admit that you have some biases and accept it as normal. Second, understand that it is to a great extent correctable. If you want to rise above your peers, question your core beliefs. Some core beliefs might need to be painfully discarded, but it is an exercise in humility that will produce a clearer, more logical reasoning process. Third, learn to identify facts in a non-judgmental way. Start with small things. Did someone cut in front of you in traffic? Instead of saying "That maniac cut in front of me," say, "That car cut in front of me." The "maniac" part is just an opinion unless you happen to know it by getting more information.

How to Use Biases and Fantasies to Your Advantage

Recognize that over-familiarity increases contempt

There is truth to the saying, "Familiarity breeds contempt." No wonder that this saying dates back at least 2000 years. Be careful not to make yourself too familiar to others. The closer the mirror, the more defects become apparent. Familiarity can make you seem ordinary, predictable and boring to others. Have good boundaries with others and always keep at least a little bit of your mind private. It is better to keep a little distance and be appreciated than to bare your soul and be disrespected.

Avoid disclosing too many of your thoughts and feelings to others. If there is no mystery to you and you are 100% transparent, what need do others have to be around you? You are a known quantity: boring, with nothing new to contribute. Keep your distance a little bit from others and do not disclose everything about you to anyone. Good boundaries are protective and there are some things you probably do not even have to tell your closest confidants. The further away someone is from being a close family member or friend, the less they should know about you. If you have little to share with others and are at risk of becoming boring, start learning new things and find new experiences to talk and connect about with other people.

Avoid getting pigeon-holed

Do not be tied to specifics about everything—opinions, preferences, etc. Having all kinds of specific likes and dislikes will alienate you from people, except a minority that shares your exact point of view. It is tempting in social media to "like" or promote all kinds of narrow opinions because you believe they are true, but this will cause some useful people to shun you when they disagree. Besides, you are not likely to really influence others who already have their own fixed beliefs and opinions. Specific political and religious ideas will distance you from many people. There are fewer opportunities within a small pool of people than a large pool. The less settled you are in your ways, the more people will be comfortable including you in their world. The murkier the image, the more people see what they want to see. Many politicians have been successful using this strategy; the less detail they provide about their positions, the more people will think they agree with them because of the absence of a contradiction. But very specific opinions are the most divisive. It usually does not hurt, but helps when other people see that you are not the opposite of them.

Resist the fantasy that you can always trust systems for protection

One fantasy common to people is that society safeguards us from harm and that our leaders can be trusted. Maybe in some societies this is true most of the time, but it is never true 100 percent of the time. You might find yourself in a position where the systems in place do not protect you from injustice, unfairness or hostility. Unfortunately, good people sometimes put too much faith in "systems," like legal protections, ethics policies, and human resources investigations. The powers that be are sometimes undermined by bias and favoritism, which means using them can be risky. No one will admit a bias; instead, they will use excuses to procrastinate or even turn on someone with a legitimate grievance, labeling them a "complainer." When systems are biased or dysfunctional, any pursuit of justice is doomed from the beginning and the effort expended will be a waste of time and energy. For some, job security and the opinions of superiors are much more important than justice and fairness.

The greater the power, the more dangerous the abuse.
—Edmund Burke

Consider a lesson from history. The ancient Roman historian Suetonius recorded that the emperor Tiberius began his career with intelligence and merit, but upon becoming emperor slowly devolved into a sadistic man who terrorized and murdered countless innocent individuals. Tiberius, however, usually tried to find some legal pretext to justify his crimes. In one instance he wanted to execute a woman but could not legally justify the action because it was against the law to corporally punish a virgin. One of his supporters suggested that the solution was to have her "deflowered so she could be devoured." Taking this advice, Tiberius ordered that the girl be raped, and afterwards executed. This unfortunate kind of event—where the law was used for harm rather than protection—has been common in the history of humanity. The law of the land can be a meager source of protection against strong-willed and powerful persons who manipulate it for their own benefit or cast it aside entirely when it interferes with their objectives.

So what is to be done when our ordinary protections, like the law or an organization's policies, do not protect us from a powerful or influential person? There are really only three ways to respond:

1) Find an advocate or allies that will provide assistance; for example, a minority group that shares your concerns or has also been wronged.

2) Risk being a "pest" by not giving up. Eventually you might get what you want because others are tired of expending time and energy on your situation. Accept the possibility that you could be marginalized and subtly persecuted.

3) Throw in the towel, call it a loss, and move on with your life.

Leaders often cannot be trusted, despite appearances

Figuratively speaking, Tiberius is alive today. There is a "type" of individual who is like him, but without absolute power. It may be frightening to believe, but there are many individuals who might appear to be respectable, but are capable of becoming monsters when given even a little bit of power. In the modern, Western world such individuals are not likely to try to take your life, but when given the chance, they will seek to dominate and intimidate you. Even the mayor of a small town can have the ego of a Mussolini. But the other extreme is also true: there are always some individuals able to help many other people if given the chance. In most cases, you will never know what someone—including yourself—is truly capable of doing in highly unusual situations. This does not mean that someone who is capable of being a monster actually *is* some kind of monster. Possessing a lot of power over others or experiencing extreme suffering are abnormal experiences that human beings cannot usually manage without risk of losing our moral bearing. We are not hard-wired to endure extremes. To use an analogy, an animal that is by nature sociable and content can easily become aggressive if threatened or injured; on the other hand, many animals, if given unlimited treats, will succumb to inactivity and obesity. These responses are hardly the fault of the animal. *Animals, like humans, are not designed by nature to cope with the extremes of intense suffering OR excessive gratification.* Human beings find it difficult to manage great power because it provides opportunities for excessive gratification.

Understand that a person's true character is like energy: it flows with the least resistance and the better the conduit, the greater the flow. When selfish individuals have limited power, little harm can be done on a wide scale; however, when selfish individuals have great power, there is likely to be harm to anyone opposing them. Under modern democratic governments you are not likely to ever encounter someone with absolute power, but you will meet many for whom even a little bit of power results in feelings of entitlement or an attitude of superiority. The abuse of power takes many forms, but in the end, it is just an attempt to dominate others. If you find yourself a target of the abuse of power, you must learn how to respond optimally. Hostility, excessive criticism, marginalization, or other attempts to dominate you require swift and decisive responses. If you wait too long to respond, you will find yourself demoralized and unable to improve your situation.

The true character of a person at the deepest level—what the religious call "souls"—seldom manifests itself for all to see. Life generally allows us to operate on autopilot as we avoid the extremes of unbridled desire and great suffering. This homeostasis is sometimes broken by a pivotal event, such as a personal crisis or critical opportunity that requires us to make difficult decisions. For some, these kinds of experiences reveal what is at the core of our being. Thankfully, most of life is predictable and we are seldom tested on a core level. Be sure to notice how people respond in unusual circumstances to assess their character.

Summary

Understanding how the human mind makes judgments about things is like carrying a sword and a shield. Knowing about biases and the underlying psychology of power is advantageous and can take your understanding of human behavior to a higher level. You can use this knowledge to protect yourself and influence others. Self-knowledge about biases is especially useful; it allows us to correct illogical tendencies resulting in greater objectivity, fairness, and ethical decision-making.

Taking Inventory

Ask yourself...

- Can you accept that people are heavily influenced by fantasies?
- Are you able to recognize how common biases are in human psychology?
- Do you recognize that there is usually a gap between how people view themselves and how others perceive them?

Change Something

Do things differently...

- Do not let yourself be taken for granted by becoming overly familiar with others.
- Acknowledge and recognize your own biases to put a check on them and think more logically.
- Use the biases of others to your advantage.

Develop Wisdom

Consider that...

- The human mind tries to protect us from psychological pain with irrational defenses.
- Heightened self-awareness is a huge advantage.
- It is not wise to automatically trust leaders and established systems for protection.
- Self-correction about core assumptions is hard, but critical to success.

Chapter 12

Law 12: Be Conspicuous or Risk Getting Overlooked

If you don't get noticed, you don't have anything. You just have to be noticed, but the art is in getting noticed naturally, without screaming or without tricks.

—Leo Burnett

If you are competent, work hard, and produce good outcomes, it does not follow that others will necessarily notice, care, or reward you. In a perfect world this might be true, but to be truly successful you need to engage the world as it is, not as it should be. Start by replacing the thought that "People should notice me" with the thought "How can I get people to notice me?" No matter how much you believe in the virtue of humility there are key times when you need to call attention to yourself or risk getting ignored. Getting noticed does not imply arrogance—it is sometimes a necessity on the path to career promotion and effective social engagement. Of course you should avoid the opposite extreme—calling too much attention to yourself, or people will resent you for appearing conceited. Thus a middle path is best, but this requires artful execution.

Merit is not enough by itself because it competes with social likeability and gregariousness for attention. Even a top performer is likely to be sidelined in favor of someone who does not excel in other areas but has a winning personality. This is especially true within interpersonal relationships. A romantic partner, friend, or family member is likely to prioritize the quality of a relationship over just about anything else, including how responsible, disciplined, or generous you might be. If you cannot connect with others with affection, fun, or conversation, you are likely to remain lonely.

The Student Analogy

The idea that merit is not always enough to get noticed can first be noticed in youth. The 4.0 student that is highly introverted is not likely to get as much positive attention as the 3.5 student that is highly sociable. The student body president is seldom a total bookworm. On the other end of the spectrum, the "trouble-makers" often get much more attention than students who do not break the rules. These circumstances are not terribly different from what adults experience in their relationships and careers. Quiet people of merit seldom get rewarded to the same extent as those of slightly less merit who are more sociable. In order to achieve one's goals it is therefore usually necessary to be social, likeable, interested in others, and willing to ask for feedback about how other people think you are doing. The ideal formula for getting noticed is merit + sociability + ethics. The perception of holding to ethical standards is important too because it brings trust.

Get Noticed at Work

At work one of the most obvious ways to get positive attention is to exceed the stated goals set by your employer and get recognized for it. For example, imagine a placement specialist who was told to attain seven placements in a month. That employee could vastly exceed that expectation and achieve double or more the stated placements every month. If this kind of accomplishment is not noticed, then the employee should ask for a meeting with his or her manager and say something like, "I have more than doubled our placement objectives for the last two quarters; I would like to know if there are advancement opportunities that I could pursue?" This would be a statement of fact combined with a question that conveys a healthy ambition; moreover, it allows the person to get information about his or her potential. Chances are that by planting that seed the manager could at some future point ask the employee to take on other tasks or offer a promotion.

Call Attention to Yourself without Arrogance

Call attention to yourself without being perceived as a braggart by getting to know whoever is in charge of media releases or news stories about your interests. Connect with someone who can help you pitch an idea about an article on a topic that they may find of interest that happens to feature a project you are working on. If you are successful, the article will not only feature your project but mention you and your organization in a positive light.

Use Social Media

Currently we live in a culture dominated by smartphones, computers, digital media and the internet. Communication via social media such as Facebook, Instagram, Snapchat, LinkedIn, Twitter, Digg and several career-related websites are critical in the contemporary world. Those who know how to navigate and use these types of websites to their advantage will benefit while those who do not will not be as easily accessible and will therefore be frequently ignored, usually without even knowing about it. At a minimum, make sure you are at least savvy to the major internet websites and willing to communicate on them if need be. Throughout the world billions use these sites for the profit of their businesses and exposure to new clientele.

You Plus Pleasure = Desirability

One way to ensure that you are not overlooked is to be associated with pleasure. Nearly every living animal on this planet seeks pleasure and avoids pain, including humans. If you can get others to associate you with pleasure they will appreciate your company. The inverse is also true: few will cherish your presence if you primarily exude negativity. If you can get others to associate your presence with positive feelings you will find yourself more liked, included, and sought out more than others. Do not be like the smug pessimists who think that they will be respected because they are sometimes "right" about problems. Most people want to have hope about the future and see things in a positive light and they will eventually dread someone who goes around deflating their expectations. On the other hand, excessive optimism or cheerfulness is usually considered annoying and superficial. The best social appeal is to appear as if you possess sound judgment about the harsh realities of life while simultaneously making others feel at ease about their problems. There are four general ways of communicating that are crucial to making this approach successful: *skillful complimenting; reframing the negative; identifying future possibilities*, and *providing tangible feedback*.

Skillful complimenting

Make it your habit to skillfully compliment others. *Skillfully* means that your compliments are *brief, specific, occur at the right time, and are perceived as genuine*. Each of these approaches is essential to maximizing your effect upon others. Avoid being effusive or too general. Saying someone is "fabulous" or "wonderful" over and over will quickly make you lose credibility. Lengthy praise and undeserved compliments are not taken seriously and will lead others to assume that you either have a personality defect or an agenda to ingratiate yourself with their goodwill. Be succinct and make it personal, then move on to the next subject like it is no big deal. This is a very subtle effort in that it may appear as though the other person was not impressed, but remember, appearances are not reality. Most people are so caught up in their own self-criticism and experience such little praise from others that they will at the very least be appreciative of your good nature.

Reframe the negative by highlighting the positive

Help assuage guilt and negative feelings by reframing the negative into a positive. Begin by acknowledging difficult facts but quickly move into identifying the one positive thing about the situation—even if it is minor. Nearly anything can be reframed or shaped attitudinally by suggesting another perspective. This is easier than you might think because people are generally eager to avoid the suffering of a painful situation or memory and desire to have their hopes restored. You can help them by pointing out how good their intentions were and that there was at least some minor positive outcome, regardless of difficulties.

When the past is painful, point out future possibilities

While the past consists of memories, the future is uncertain. It is human nature to shun difficult memories and focus on future hopes. You can make use of this predilection by identifying a reason to be hopeful about the future. In some circumstances it might be a stretch, but again, this will seem credible if you are specific and begin by acknowledging the reality of any problems. Avoid lack of specificity, e.g. saying that "Somehow it will all work out" or communicating platitudes that cause others to view your words as meaningless.

Example of the method

Karen described how difficult it was to fire a long-term employee, but said that corporate gave her no choice. Joe listened carefully and replied that although it was unfortunate that the employee had to be terminated [acknowledgment of reality], *the way she did it was very tactful and professional* [compliment]. *Besides, he added, the department probably needed some new blood* [highlighting the positive] *and now she has a great opportunity to hire someone who could really benefit the department* [instilling hope for future possibilities].

Implementing this approach does not imply brushing aside harsh realities. Always acknowledge in a realistic way that you understand the nature of the problem before isolating or reframing into the positive. Do not rush to expect any personal advantage. This is a technique that accumulates like adding pennies to a bank account. One day or one week of being associated with positivity is unlikely to bear fruit, but if you are consistent, over time social doors will open for you that are shut for others who are more negative or neutral than positive.

Provide tangible feedback

Finally, becoming associated with pleasure should involve rewarding others with tangible things. This should be done *carefully* because you do not want to be defined as a "gift giver" or identified as someone attempting to curry the favor of others. In most Western cultures a "thank you" card or small gift might suffice. Generally speaking, your gifts or notes should be special enough to convey that you put some thought into the effort. *It is critical that you do not do this on a regular basis.* What becomes expected eventually becomes commonplace and loses its impact. This approach can be used with anyone, but it will do the most good when directed toward those above you in an organizational hierarchy. It is not terribly important whether you are associated with pleasure among those distant from you in a hierarchy. Avoid being generous if you think someone is prone to misinterpreting it as an attempt to placate their unhappiness.

The Social Cost of Negativity

There are always many negative people in organizations. The pessimists, complainers, and gossipers look for others to commiserate with in private in order to justify their grievances. Their negative communication serves as a farce for intimacy that for a brief moment bonds them in their shared unhappiness. But this is a weak bond. Meaningful relationships are never built on misery, but upon trust, respect, and positive shared interests. The lure of negative people is that in truth there are usually many legitimate things to be unhappy about in any relationship, organization, or circumstance, but do not be tempted to indulge yourself in futile exchanges about weakness and defeat. If you become one of them you will find that the truly ambitious and successful people in the world will avoid you because naturally they expect negativity from negative people, not success.

Do not go out of your way to entirely avoid interacting with complainers and pessimists. Despite their poor attitudes, many of them usually have other qualities that may make them competitive or draw others to them. In such circumstances, you must placate them without justifying everything they say. The meta-communication you want to convey should be something like, "I understand your grievances and I am not against you. Sometimes I will listen. But I am going to focus on the positive and give little time to focusing upon negativity."

It is important to note that everything written on this subject has nothing to do with what you actually feel or believe about a situation. Maybe you consider yourself a pessimist, cynic, or skeptic, but the subject at hand is not about sharing your world-view; it is about how your actions impact others. You can believe anything you want to believe, but remember that in the realm of relational power your success depends upon using your time wisely and shaping the perceptions of others to maximum effect.

The above approach does not necessarily involve deceit of any kind. Consider that life is already filled with enough negativity and that many people are highly self-critical. If you can help them reframe their perspectives about themselves and their problems then you are just balancing the scales by selectively highlighting the positive. As an analogy, there would be nothing wrong with hating a painting, but nonetheless taking the time to carefully notice one tiny aspect of it to your liking.

Taking Inventory

Ask yourself…

- Are you waiting around to get noticed?
- Do others who have less merit than you seem to get all the attention?
- Are you uncomfortable calling attention to your accomplishments?

Change Something

Do things differently…

- Be associated with pleasure to increase likeability.
- Avoid appearing conceited by asking for feedback about performance in a matter-of-fact way.
- Use social media to your advantage.

Develop Wisdom

Consider that…

- Merit is only one piece of what it takes to be successful.
- Excessive humility and arrogance are self-defeating extremes.
- Negative people with desirable qualities should be managed rather than shunned.
- There is already a lot of negativity in the world and therefore little need to add to it.

Chapter 13

Law 13: Good Intentions Do Not Excuse Bad Behavior

The evil that is in the world almost always comes of ignorance, and good intentions may do as much harm as malevolence if they lack understanding.
— Albert Camus

Trust Intentions at Your Own Risk

Should bad behavior, mistakes, or accidents be excused when after-the-fact someone apologizes and claims they had good intentions? Are there times when truly good intentions are *not* a good excuse to let someone off the hook? How do you really know when someone has good intentions? If you do not know the answer to these questions you are at risk for exploitation by those who will interpret your willingness to forgive or forget as a free pass to get away with actions that cause problems for you. When you accept excuses from people whenever they claim "good intentions," you will at some point find yourself manipulated by those who think that they can get away with anything as long as they get you to buy into their excuses. This kind of manipulation typically results in resentment, burnout, and a feeling of powerlessness about how to change the situation.

Consider the following examples of actions possibly based upon good intentions that cause problems for other people:

- Trying to *help* someone, but in the effort making the situation worse
- Trying to *accomplish* something, but doing it carelessly so that it fails
- Cutting corners to be *efficient*, resulting in mistakes

- *Perfectionism* at the expense of time and efficiency
- Controlling or intimidating others to *motivate* them
- Promoting the *truth* by arguing someone to death
- Helping someone to *improve* with repetitive criticism
- Trying to *protect* someone by hiding the truth
- Trying to *learn* about something by getting private information without permission

Notice that the above words at face value indicate positive intentions: *protect*; *help*; *accomplish*; *learn*, etc. but they each involve accomplishing something using problematic methods. Someone can say they did this or that to try to "help" or "motivate" you, but this could easily be an excuse for selfish behavior. For example, if a person wanted to stonewall a project with procrastination, they could claim that they are being slow to make sure they do a task correctly and without mistakes. Even hostile behavior can sometimes also be concealed with supposedly good intentions. Imagine someone wanting to demoralize you with the mixed message, "I really respect you, so I will confide in you that a lot of people dislike you. They don't want you to get the promotion." The appearance of good intentions is often a mask for selfish intentions.

Pizza analogy

Even when you can confirm good intentions, they are not necessarily enough to excuse undesirable behavior. If you went to a restaurant and ordered a pizza, but the chef instead brought you a salad, would it make any difference if he said, "But trust me, I care that you eat healthy and a salad is better for you than pizza"? More than likely you would not want that chef to cook for you anymore. This is because actions are more important than intentions. This is especially true when it comes to the things that matter most to us in life. *Good intentions are not good enough. Even wars can be justified by good intentions.*

Another problem with intentions is that they are often murky. Someone can have bad intentions and claim otherwise. Someone can have good intentions, but make mistakes. There are also mixed intentions—like when someone does not want to harm you but is only half-heartedly concerned about how an outcome personally impacts you when it really counts. Another possibility is that someone might have good intentions, but only until some selfish temptation comes along. Unless you know someone very well, you cannot get a sense of their inner psyche to make a good guess about internal motivations. Unless you are a gifted mind-reader, you can never hope to know what someone else is actually thinking, *but you do know their actions*. It is just better, generally speaking, to focus on actions (which you can see) rather than intentions (which are hidden).

Even when someone has acceptable motives it can exclude any concern about you. "Good for the organization" may not mean "good for you," and "good for our relationship" may not mean "it is in your best interest." People tend to put a positive spin on what they want to do or have done to get others to accept it. It is not selfish to accept that even noble motivations should not necessarily exclude your needs and desires.

Here are some guidelines to help you determine the importance of intentions versus actions:

Determine whether someone has considered alternative actions

Imagine a husband saying to his wife, "Of course I use cocaine. I know it's illegal, but my intentions are good. It helps me focus, gives me energy, and I lose weight." This argument fails because it excludes other, less harmful solutions to increase energy and lose weight. When someone has alternatives to a bad decision, but acted in a way that harmed you regardless, they are probably just using excuses to justify doing what they wanted to do.

Ask yourself, "How bad was the behavior?"

The more negative the consequences, the greater the accountability. Many catastrophes, such as plane crashes and shipwrecks, have been caused by unintentional, erratic driving, resulting in loss of life. Rarely does an intoxicated driver intend to harm someone else, but when they do, the consequences are so terrible (death or injury) that the absence of bad intentions is no excuse for harm. When someone causes you problems, determine how its severity impacted you. The rule of thumb is: the more severe the consequences, the less intentions matter.

Look for patterns

If someone has a pattern of causing you problems, but they always seem to have an excuse equivalent to "I'm sorry, I didn't mean to," then there is a strong possibility that they are not making a good-faith effort to avoid causing you problems. Carelessness and negligence are offenses no less than bad intent. People that know in advance what *could* happen, but ignore precautions, are culpable. It would not make sense for someone to claim, "I never make my child wear a seatbelt, but I didn't do anything wrong. Sure, my child got hurt, but the odds were against getting in a car accident today, so I should be let off the hook."

Recognize that intentions are relative

Good intentions are relative to a person's point of view. Criminal offenders sometimes sincerely think it is just fine to steal from someone because the other person had something they wanted, e.g. "Yeah, I stole from my dad, but you don't understand, I really needed a fix. My dad is rich and won't miss it anyhow. I was just trying to avoid withdrawals!" Avoid entitled people that act like their needs are excuses for anything.

Accept that those with harmful intentions seldom disclose what they are really thinking

Virtually any bad behavior can be spun to be based upon positive intentions, especially when the tables are turned and the victim is getting blamed. Was your wife unfaithful? Well, she is so sorry, but she did not get enough attention. Did your supervisor scream profanities at you in anger? Well, he was only upset because he wants the best for the company. Did someone lie to you—it must have been to protect you. Let others know that you do not accept bad behavior, regardless of excuses.

Notice when good intentions fail due to poor judgment

Imagine reading the following story in a newspaper:

> The Mayor of the City of Clover wanted to encourage reading among children in grade school. He provided 50 free books with six different titles for children to pick out and read. One of the book titles was *A History of Serial Killers in Graphic Detail.*

Okay, perhaps no reasonable mayor would do such a thing, but do not miss the point: *good intentions make things worse unless they are accompanied by good judgment.* In the example just given, while encouraging children to read is a good idea, someone with bad judgment might pick out an inappropriate book. Ask yourself whether someone in your life has such poor judgment about certain things that they cannot be trusted, regardless of their good intentions toward you.

Testing Intentions

There are of course times when someone has a legitimate excuse to the extent that we cannot justify blame or suspicion. Consider the following instances where it is usually acceptable to excuse mistakes and problems:

- When someone is new to something and is still learning
- When someone is genuinely misinformed or ignorant, and there was no obvious reason for them to consider alternatives
- When you know someone's character and you can trust them not to exploit a situation
- When something is trivial
- When there is genuine remorse and no pattern of problems
- When someone has a legitimate personal problem or disability that impairs their judgment

Scrutinize Your Own Intentions

The intention to help others at great expense leaves no winners

Just as we need to put more weight on someone's actions than on excuses—even good excuses—others will usually care more about how our actions impact them than how "sorry" we feel. Do not expect others to appreciate your good intentions over the impact your actions have upon them. Consider the following scenario:

Tina put a lot of her own money into a start-up web-developing business. Due to her contacts in the industry she quickly got a few contracts and hired three women she knew from the business. Over time, they became friends and sometimes went out together after work. Then the Great Recession hit. Two big contracts were lost. She was appalled when her accountant told her that she was losing money and needed to cut expenses. Tina told all the employees that she cares for them, wants the business to succeed, and only out of necessity will be cutting their salaries. She was shocked when the employees started avoiding her and spreading nasty rumors about her; after all, she had good intentions and was trying to do the right thing.

Tina did nothing wrong—she was just trying to save the business and not lay anyone off. However, she underestimated the tendency people have to focus more upon how actions negatively impact them over good intentions. Of course not everyone would act like her employees; on the other hand, it is not uncommon.

Another scenario involves actions based on good intentions, but in an OCD and perfectionistic manner that causes problems for others. In the follow scenario, Cassie sabotaged the very job she wanted to keep because of the hardships she created for others:

Cassie was a paralegal who worked for a local attorney. In order to protect herself from criticism and ensure job security, she learned to explain everything in lengthy, detailed emails, and called him about anything she was about to do that could go wrong. This protected her because whenever she was blamed she could pull out an old email or inform him that he had actually asked her to do something. Her intention was understandable—to protect herself from getting fired. The problem is that her lengthy emails and frequent phone calls drove the attorney crazy, stressed him out, and distracted him from his job. He told Cassie to cut down on all the communication, but Cassie thought it was a plot to fire her and kept it up. Cassie's intention to keep her job and not make mistakes was superficially innocent, but the effect was annoying. Cassie was eventually fired for this repetitive behavior.

In the above examples, genuinely good intentions actually got in the way of professional interpersonal relationships.

People with high morals and sensitive consciences tend to be over-concerned with their intentions and how their actions might impact others. This causes them to second-guess themselves and become mired in excessive self-scrutiny, which erodes self-confidence. Conversely, selfish people do the opposite: they tend to blame others or take on the role of a victim, even when they are the ones that perpetrated harm. The best of us can get caught up in over-emphasizing the importance of intentions. Thus there is much truth in the saying, "Good people tend to think they are evil, while the evil often think that they are good." Break free from the mind-trap of self-doubt by focusing upon your actions, which people care about most, rather than getting hung up with self-scrutiny.

Taking Inventory

Ask yourself...

- Do you excuse problems and mistakes just because someone claims to have meant well?
- Do you feel manipulated by the excuses people give to get away with things?
- Do you know how to discern good intentions versus excuses for bad behavior?

Change Something

Do something different...

- Look for patterns of behavior to discern manipulation.
- Put more weight on actions than words and expect the same from yourself.
- Test someone's intentions before you believe them.

Develop Wisdom

Consider that...

- Good intentions fail without good judgment.
- Few selfish individuals ever admit their motives and instead claim good intentions.
- Even wars start with claimed good intentions.

CHANGE
MAKERS
BOOKS

Changemakers Books
TRANSFORMATION

Transform your life, transform your world - Changemakers Books publishes for individuals committed to transforming their lives and transforming the world. Our readers seek to become positive, powerful agents of change. Changemakers Books inform, inspire, and provide practical wisdom and skills to empower us to write the next chapter of humanity's future.
If you have enjoyed this book, why not tell other readers by posting a review on your preferred book site. Recent bestsellers from Changemakers Books are:

Integration
The Power of Being Co-Active in Work and Life
Ann Betz, Karen Kimsey-House
Integration examines how we came to be polarized in our dealing with self and other, and what we can do to move from an either/or state to a more effective and fulfilling way of being.
Paperback: 978-1-78279-865-1 ebook: 978-1-78279-866-8

Bleating Hearts
The Hidden World of Animal Suffering
Mark Hawthorne
An investigation of how animals are exploited for entertainment, apparel, research, military weapons, sport, art, religion, food, and more.
Paperback: 978-1-78099-851-0 ebook: 978-1-78099-850-3

Lead Yourself First!
Indispensable Lessons in Business and in Life
Michelle Ray
Are you ready to become the leader of your own life? Apply simple, powerful strategies to take charge of yourself, your career, your destiny.
Paperback: 978-1-78279-703-6 ebook: 978-1-78279-702-9

Burnout to Brilliance
Strategies for Sustainable Success
Jayne Morris
Routinely running on reserves? This book helps you transform your life from burnout to brilliance with strategies for sustainable success.
Paperback: 978-1-78279-439-4 ebook: 978-1-78279-438-7

Goddess Calling
Inspirational Messages & Meditations of Sacred Feminine Liberation Thealogy
Rev. Dr. Karen Tate
A book of messages and meditations using Goddess archetypes and mythologies, aimed at educating and inspiring those with the desire to incorporate a feminine face of God into their spirituality.
Paperback: 978-1-78279-442-4 ebook: 978-1-78279-441-7

The Master Communicator's Handbook
Teresa Erickson, Tim Ward
Discover how to have the most communicative impact in this guide by professional communicators with over 30 years of experience advising leaders of global organizations.
Paperback: 978-1-78535-153-2 ebook: 978-1-78535-154-9

Meditation in the Wild
Buddhism's Origin in the Heart of Nature
Charles S. Fisher Ph.D.
A history of Raw Nature as the Buddha's first teacher, inspiring
some followers to retreat there in search of truth.
Paperback: 978-1-78099-692-9 ebook: 978-1-78099-691-2

Ripening Time
Inside Stories for Aging with Grace
Sherry Ruth Anderson
Ripening Time gives us an indispensable guidebook for growing
into the deep places of wisdom as we age.
Paperback: 978-1-78099-963-0 ebook: 978-1-78099-962-3

Striking at the Roots
A Practical Guide to Animal Activism
Mark Hawthorne
A manual for successful animal activism from an author with
first-hand experience speaking out on behalf of animals.
Paperback: 978-1-84694-091-0 ebook: 978-1-84694-653-0

Voices of the Sacred Feminine
Conversations to Re-Shape Our World
Rev. Dr. Karen Tate
If we can envision it, we can manifest it! Discover conversations
that help us begin to re-shape the world!
Paperback: 978-1-78279-510-0 ebook: 978-1-78279-509-4

Readers of ebooks can buy or view any of these bestsellers by clicking on the live link in the title. Most titles are published in paperback and as an ebook. Paperbacks are available in traditional bookshops. Both print and ebook formats are available online.

Find more titles and sign up to our readers' newsletter at
http://www.johnhuntpublishing.com/transformation
Follow us on Facebook at
https://www.facebook.com/Changemakersbooks

MODERN MACHIAVELLI will teach you smart, social tactics to advan[ce] your career and improve your relationships. This book explains how [to] successfully manage conflict, influence others, and understand the ove[rt] and covert dynamics of interpersonal power. It challenges false but common[ly] held beliefs that undermine personal and career success. Master the unwritt[en] rules of the social game that few understand.

"This is a book about how to swim with the sharks while living like a dolphin[.] It provides a unique mix of cunning and integrity – as if Machiavelli and Stephen Covey got together and wrote a book on the rules for living. Withou[t] being either pessimistic or cynical, the book deals with some hard truths about human nature that we ignore at our peril. The authors' advice is both practical and tactical on topics such as dealing with conflict, office politics, difficult personalities, and not letting others take advantage of you. Master these techniques and you'll be adept at handling the worst in others, while strengthening what's best in yourself."
TIM WARD, author of *Indestructible You* and *The Master Communicator's Handbook*

"Every person experiencing interpersonal conflict or cut-throat competition should read this book. I have personally benefited from Dr. Bruner's consultation and highly recommend his book. It is the opposite of psycho-babble: concrete, specific, and dynamic."
ROBERT W. FORSTER, President and CEO, Forster Financial

"*Modern Machiavelli* provides key insights and inspiration to propel your life dramatically forward!"
WILLIAM EAGER, speaker, corporate strategist and best-selling author

"Dr. Bruner and Philip Eager have provided a much needed treatise on the basic behavioral "laws" that all of us need to fully understand. This book is not designed to show you how to manipulate co-workers, friends and family members, but rather provides the reader with a strategic awareness of the many facets that may be in play when individuals interact, regardless of the situation. This book is a must for the reader who is interested in a layman's dive into moral development and offers approaches through professional insights and examples about how to succeed without compromising our core values that make us who we are."
DAVID WHITE, PH.D., Associate Dean of Research, University of Tennessee

"*Modern Machiavelli: 13 Laws of Power, Persuasion and Integrity* is a book tha[t] crosses the areas of business, psychology, self-help and ethics. It is a realist'[s] manual for effective persuasion and conflict management."
CHRISTINE JOO, ED.D., Clinical Psychologist

www.changemakers-books.com

Change Makers Books

BODY, MIND & SPIRIT
UK £11.99
US $18.95

Cover image © Adobe Stock
Cover design by Design Deluxe

US $18.95
ISBN 978-1-78535-611-7

9 781785 356117